THE TARJUMÁN AL-ASHWÁQ

THE TARJUMÁN AL-ASHWÁQ

A COLLECTION OF MYSTICAL ODES

MUHYI'DDIN IBN AL-'ARABI;

EDITED FROM THREE MANUSCRIPTS WITH A LITERAL TRANSLATION OF THE TEXT AND AN ABRIDGED VERSION OF THE AUTHOR'S COMMENTARY

GYAN

Published by

Gyan Publishing House
5, Ansari Road
Daryaganj, New Delhi-110002
Phone: 011-47034999, 9811692060
E-mail: books@gyanbooks.com

Distribution Network
gyanbooks.com
India, USA, Canada, UK, Australia

ISBN: 978-93-7225-500-3 (HB)

First Published, 1911

2nd Impression 2025

Printed at: Gyan Press, Delhi.

THE TARJUMÁN AL-ASHWÁQ
Arthur: MUHYI'DDIN IBN AL-'ARABI

ORIENTAL TRANSLATION FUND.

NEW SERIES.

VOL. XX.

THE TARJUMÁN AL-ASHWÁQ

A COLLECTION OF MYSTICAL ODES

BY

MUḤYI'DDÍN IBN AL-'ARABÍ

EDITED FROM THREE MANUSCRIPTS WITH A LITERAL VERSION OF THE TEXT AND AN ABRIDGED TRANSLATION OF THE AUTHOR'S COMMENTARY THEREON

BY

REYNOLD A. NICHOLSON, M.A., LITT.D.

LECTURER IN PERSIAN IN THE UNIVERSITY OF CAMBRIDGE, AND FORMERLY FELLOW OF TRINITY COLLEGE.

LONDON:

ROYAL ASIATIC SOCIETY,

22 ALBEMARLE STREET.

1911

PREFACE

WHATEVER view may be taken of the respective merits of Arabic and Persian poetry, I think it will generally be allowed by those familiar with the mystical literature of both nations that the Arabs excel in prose rather than in verse, while the Persian prose-writers on this subject cannot be compared with the poets. Farídu'ddín 'Aṭṭár, Jalálu'ddín Rúmí, Ḥáfiẓ, and Jámí—to mention only a few of the great Persian poets whose works, translated into various languages, have introduced the religious philosophy of Ṣúfiism to a rapidly widening circle of European culture—are as much superior to their Arab rivals, including even the admirable Ibn al-Fáriḍ, as the *Futúḥát al-Makkiyya* and the *Fuṣúṣ al-Ḥikam* are superior to similar treatises in Persian. The *Tarjumán al-Ashwáq* is no exception to this rule. The obscurity of its style and the strangeness of its imagery will satisfy those austere spirits for whom literature provides a refined and arduous form of intellectual exercise, but the sphere in which the author moves is too abstract and remote from common experience to give pleasure to others who do not share his visionary temper or have not themselves drawn inspiration from the same order of ideas. Nevertheless, the work of such a bold and subtle genius deserves, at any rate, to be studied, and students will find, as a reward for their labour, many noble and striking thoughts and some passages of real beauty. The following lines are often quoted. They express the Ṣúfí doctrine that all ways lead to the One God.

'My heart has become capable of every form; it is a pasture for gazelles and a convent for Christian monks,
And a temple for idols and the pilgrim's Ka'ba and the tables of the Tora and the book of the Koran.
I follow the religion of Love: whatever way Love's camels take, that is my religion and my faith.'[1]

[1] xii, 13-15.

The present edition was designed in the first instance for the Journal of the Royal Asiatic Society, and is now published in its original shape. I will not repeat or expand what I have said in my brief introduction concerning the date of composition, the different recensions of the text, the method of interpretation, and the general character of these remarkable odes, but it may be useful to indicate in a few words some of the principal theories which are shadowed forth symbolically in the text and revealed more explicitly in the author's commentary. Although the *Tarjumán al-Ashwáq* affords material for an essay on Ibn al-'Arabí's theosophy, I feel, speaking for myself, that further study of his works is necessary before such a task can be attempted with advantage. Much valuable information is contained in a treatise on Monism by 'Alí b. Sulṭán Muḥammad al-Qárí al-Harawí [1]—a polemic directed against Ibn al-'Arabí and his followers who held that all Being is essentially one with God, notwithstanding its apparent diversity. This pamphlet was written in answer to a champion of Ibn al-'Arabí, who had collected under twenty-four heads various passages in the *Futúḥát* and the *Fuṣúṣ*, to which objection was taken by orthodox theologians, and had endeavoured to justify the author against his critics. 'Alí al-Qárí regards Ibn al-'Arabí as a dangerous infidel and gives him no quarter. Of course the offending passages admit of more than one interpretation, and the author would doubtless have repudiated the construction put upon them by theologians. Their pantheistic import, however, cannot be explained away. I have classified the following examples for the sake of convenience and have added a few references to the commentary on the *Tarjumán*.

1. *God and the World.* Ibn al-'Arabí says in the *Futúḥát*, 'Glory to God who brought all things into existence, being Himself their substance (اوجد الاشياء وهو عَيْنُها). He is the

[1] Brockelmann, ii, 394. The work in question is entitled رسالة فى وحدة الوجود. It appeared, together with several other tracts on the same subject, in a volume published at Constantinople in 1294 A.H., a copy of which was given to me by Dr. Riẓá Tevfíq.

substance of every object in manifestation, although He is not the substance of objects in their essences.'[1] And again, in the *Fuṣúṣ*, 'God manifests Himself in every atom of creation: He is revealed in every intelligible object and concealed from every intelligence except the intelligence of those who say that the Universe is His form and ipseity (صورته وهويته), inasmuch as He stands in the same relation to phenomenal objects as the spirit to the body.'

2. *God and Man.* 'Man is the form of God and God is the spirit of Man.' 'Man is to God as the pupil to the eye: by means of him God beholds the objects which He has created.' 'Man's origin is both temporal and eternal; he is an organism durable and everlasting.' 'Man is the substance of every attribute wherewith he endows God: when he contemplates God he contemplates himself, and God contemplates Himself when He contemplates Man. Hence Abú Sa'íd al-Kharráz said that he was a face and tongue of God, who is called by the name of Abú Sa'íd al-Kharráz and also by other temporal names, because God unites all opposites in Himself.'

God dwells in the heart of Man (vi, 1), and Man, invested with Divine qualities, is a mirror which displays God to Himself (x, 2). Divine qualities may justly be attributed to anyone who is so transported from himself that God becomes his eye and his ear (x, 1). Although union with God is not possible while the body exists (v, 2), Ibn al-'Arabí, like Plotinus, holds that 'deification' is attainable (xxiv, 3).[2] Elsewhere he says that knowledge of God is the utmost goal that can be reached by any contingent being (xvii, 5). This knowledge is gained solely by means of Faith and Contemplation, which Reason may serve if it consents to lay aside its reflective faculty (iii, 2, 5). What, then, is the end of knowledge? Apparently, a state of Nirvana or transcendental unconsciousness, الفناء عن الفناء

[1] Cf. xx, 25: 'The Divine attributes are manifested in creation, but the Divine essence does not enter into creation.'

[2] Cf. xxv, 7.

(v, 6). The phenomenal vanishes in presence of the Eternal (xx, 19).

3. *Religion.* Since all things are a manifestation of the Divine substance, it follows that God may be worshipped in a star or a calf or any other object, and that no form of positive religion contains more than a portion of the truth. 'Do not attach yourself,' Ibn al-'Arabí says, 'to any particular creed exclusively, so that you disbelieve in all the rest; otherwise you will lose much good, nay, you will fail to recognize the real truth of the matter. Let your soul be capable of embracing all forms of belief. God, the omnipresent and omnipotent, is not limited by any one creed, for He says, "Wheresoever ye turn, there is the face of Allah" (Kor. ii, 109); and the face of a thing is its reality.' It is vain to quarrel about religion. 'Everyone praises what he believes; his god is his own creature, and in praising it he praises himself. Consequently he blames the beliefs of others, which he would not do if he were just, but his dislike is based on ignorance. If he knew Junayd's saying—"the water takes its colour from the vessel containing it"—he would not interfere with the beliefs of others, but would perceive God in every form and in every belief.'[1] The Divine substance remains unchanged and unchangeable amidst all the variety of religious experience. 'Those who worship God in the sun behold a sun, and those who worship Him in living things see a living thing, and those who worship Him in inanimate objects see an inanimate object, and those who worship Him as a Being unique and unparalleled see that which has no like' (xii, 13). In a noteworthy passage Ibn al-'Arabí seeks to harmonize Islam with Christianity. The Christian Trinity, he says, is essentially a Unity which has its counterpart in the three cardinal Names whereby God is signified in the Koran, viz. Allah, ar-Raḥmán, and ar-Rabb (xii, 4). Islam is peculiarly the religion of Love (xi, 15), and God's mercy is denied to none, be he Moslem or infidel, who invokes Him in the extremity of his need. Even if it

[1] Cf. xiii, 12.

so be that the unbelievers shall remain in Hell for ever, they will at last feel its fiery torments a pleasure and delight.

Ibn al-'Arabí is said to have claimed that he was the Seal of the Saints, as Muḥammad was the Seal of the Prophets, and also that the Saints are superior to the Prophets, but it is very doubtful whether these accusations are well founded. He seems to have maintained that the Prophets, in so far as they are Saints, derive their knowledge from the Seal of the Saints, and that the Prophets in virtue of their saintship are superior to the Prophets in virtue of their prophetic dignity (cf. iv, i; xviii, 8). He does assert, however, that he had reached a spiritual degree which was not attained by any of his peers (xxiv, 4).

I desire gratefully to acknowledge the valuable assistance of Sir Charles Lyall, who read the text and translation in manuscript, and made a number of suggestions, nearly all of which I have inserted in the book while it was passing through the press. The fact that it has undergone his criticism enables me to offer it to students of Arabic poetry with more confidence than would otherwise have been possible. My thanks are due also to the Librarian of the University of Leiden, who caused two MSS. of the *Tarjumán* to be sent to Cambridge, and allowed them to remain there as long as they were required.

THE TARJUMAN AL-ASHWAQ

ALTHOUGH Ibn al-'Arabí (560–638 A.H.) is the most celebrated of all Muḥammadan mystics, the only one of his 150 extant works that has hitherto appeared in a European edition is the brief glossary of Ṣúfí technical terms (اصطلاحات) which was published by Fluegel in 1845, together with the *Ta'rífát* of Jurjání, under the title of *Definitiones theosophi Mohji-ed-dín Mohammed ben Ali vulgo Ibn Arabi dicti.* So far as I am aware, none of his books has been translated into any European language, and no trustworthy account can yet be given of his vast theosophical speculations, which produced an extraordinary impression throughout the Moslem world. By far the larger portion of his writings is in prose, but the poetical remnant includes a *Díwán* of about 450 pages (published at Búláq in 1271 A.H.) and several smaller collections. One of these is the *Tarjumán al-Ashwáq* or 'Interpreter of Desires'. The fact that it is accompanied by a commentary, in which the author himself explains the meaning of almost every verse, was the principal motive that induced me to study it; its brevity was a strong recommendation; and something, I suppose, may be attributed to my possessing an excellent MS., which, as is noted on the last page, has twice undergone collation and correction.

A curious problem of literary history is involved in the question of the date at which the poems and the commentary were composed. The MSS. of the *Tarjumán al-Ashwáq* exhibit three different recensions. The *first recension*, represented by Leiden 875 (2), Brit. Mus. 1527 [1], and Gotha 2268, contains *the poems without the commentary*. In his preface Ibn al-'Arabí refers to his arrival in Mecca in 598 A.H., and Dozy assumed—on insufficient grounds, as I shall presently show—that the poems were composed in that year. They were condemned by some devout Moslems as 'vain and amatorious', and in order to refute his critics the author issued a *second recension*, represented by Leiden 641 and Brit. Mus. 754[1], containing *the same poems with a commentary* and a new preface, in which he declares that he composed these poems, while visiting the holy places at Mecca, in the months of Rajab, Sha'bán, and Ramaḍán, 611 A.H. The *third recension* is represented by Bodl. (Uri) 1276, Munich 524[1], Berlin 7750 and 7751, and the MS. cited by Ḥájjí Khalífa (Fluegel's edition), ii, 276. It agrees with the second in giving the date of composition as 611 A.H., but includes a statement of the circumstances which caused the author to write his commentary.

My MS. seems to be unique[1] in so far as it contains the preface belonging to the first recension and also the additional statement which differentiates the third recension from the second.

Dozy, as I have said, believed that the true date of composition, namely 598 A.H., was given by the author in the preface to the first recension, and that on publishing the second recension he post-dated it by thirteen years. 'To wipe out the memory of his offence the poet not only proved by means of his commentary that Heavenly, not earthly, love was the theme that inspired him, but he also pretended that the poems were composed at a different time; by which artifice, though he could not deceive those who had read them before, he might dupe anyone who had heard people talk of them and the scandal produced by them.'[2]

Before considering the justice of Dozy's criticism it will be well to set forth the evidence more fully than he has done. I shall therefore summarize the contents of the prose sections which form an introduction to the text of the poems.

[1] Perhaps I should say 'almost unique', since Pertsch's description of Gotha 2269, which is defective at the beginning, leads me to suppose that it resembles my MS. in this particular. The Gotha MS., however, has the date 611 A.H., which is wanting in mine.

[2] *Leiden Cat.*, ii, 77. The last clause, as printed, runs: 'qui de iis deque magnâ offensione cuius causa exstiterant, fando audiverant,' i.e. 'the scandal which had produced them'. Dozy cannot have meant to write this.

1. Preface to the First Recension[1]

On his arrival at Mecca in 598 A.H. Ibn al-'Arabí found a number of scholars and divines, both male and female, whose ancestors had emigrated from Persia in the early days of Islam. He particularly mentions Makínu'ddín Abú Shujá' Záhir b. Rustam b. Abi 'r-Rajá al-Iṣbahání and his aged sister, Fakhru 'n-Nisá bint Rustam. [With the former he read the book of Abú 'Ísá at-Tirmidhí on the Apostolic Traditions. He begged Fakhru 'n-Nisá to let him hear Traditions from her, but she excused herself on the plea of her great age, saying that she wished to spend the last years of her life in devotion. She consented, however, that her brother should write for Ibn al-'Arabí, on her behalf, a general certificate (اجازة عامّة) for all the Traditions which she related; and he received a similar certificate from Makínu 'ddín himself.][2]

Makínu 'ddín had a young daughter, called Niẓám and surnamed 'Aynu 'sh-Shams wa 'l-Bahá, who was exceedingly beautiful and was renowned for her asceticism and eloquent preaching. [The author says that he would have descanted on her physical and moral perfections had he not been deterred by the weakness of human souls, which are easily corrupted, but he eulogizes her learning, literary accomplishments, and spiritual gifts.] Ibn al-'Arabí observed the nobility of her nature, which was enhanced by the society of her father and aunt. He celebrated her in the poems contained in this volume, using the erotic style and vocabulary, but he could not express even a small part of the feelings roused in him by the recollection of his love for her in past times (ولم ابلغ بذلك بعض ما تجده النفس ويثيره الانس من كريم ودّها وقديم عهدها). [Here my MS. adds: 'Nevertheless I have put into verse for her sake some of the longing thoughts suggested by those precious memories,

[1] I follow the text of my MS. The passages which occur in it, but not in the Leiden MS. 875 (2), are enclosed in square brackets. The Arabic text will be found below.

[2] Instead of the foregoing passage the Leiden MS. 875 (2) has: 'And I received a certificate from both of them.'

and I have uttered the sentiments of a yearning soul and have indicated the sincere attachment which I feel, fixing my mind on the bygone days and those scenes which her society has endeared to me' (اهتماما بالعهد القديم وإيثارا بالمجلس الكريم).] The author continues: 'Whenever I mention a name in this book I always allude to her, and whenever I mourn over an abode I mean her abode. In these poems I always signify Divine influences and spiritual revelations and sublime analogies, according to the most excellent way which we (Ṣúfís) follow . . . God forbid that readers of this book and of my other poems should think of aught unbecoming to souls that scorn evil and to lofty spirits that are attached to the things of Heaven! Amen!'

[These pages include the love-poems which I composed at Mecca, whilst visiting the holy places in the months of Rajab, Sha'bán, and Ramaḍán. In these poems I point (allegorically) to various sorts of Divine knowledge and spiritual mysteries and intellectual sciences and religious exhortations. I have used the erotic style and form of expression because men's souls are enamoured of it, so that there are many reasons why it should commend itself.]

2. Preface to the Second Recension

After giving a list of Ibn al-'Arabí's names and titles, the text proceeds as in the last paragraph within square brackets: 'These pages include the love-poems which I composed at Mecca . . . in the months of Rajab, Sha'bán, and Ramaḍán in the year 611. In these poems,' etc., without further variation.

3. Preface to the Third Recension

This is identical with the last, but contains in addition the following statement of the motives which induced the author to write his commentary.[1]

'I wrote this commentary on the Díwán entitled *Tarjumán*

[1] In some MSS. this statement does not form part of the preface, but is placed after the text and commentary. It occurs in my MS. on fol. 140*a*.

al-Ashwáq, which I composed at Mecca, at the request of my friend al-Mas'úd Abú Muḥammad Badr b. 'Abdallah al-Ḥabashí al-Khádim and al-Walad al-Bárr Shamsu 'ddín Ismá'íl b. Súdakín an-Núrí[1] in the city of Aleppo. He (Shamsu 'ddín) had heard some theologian remark that the author's declaration in the preface to the *Tarjumán* was not true, his declaration, namely, that the love-poems in this collection refer to mystical sciences and realities. "Probably," said the critic, "he adopted this device in order to protect himself from the imputation that he, a man famous for religion and piety, composed poetry in the erotic style." Shamsu 'ddin was offended by his observations and repeated them to me. Accordingly, I began to write the commentary at Aleppo, and a portion of it was read aloud in my lodging in the presence of the above-mentioned theologian and other divines by Kamálu 'ddín Abu 'l-Qásim b. Najmu 'ddín the Cadi Ibn al-'Adím[2]—God bless him! I finished it with difficulty and in an imperfect manner, for I was in haste to continue my journey, on the date already mentioned.[3] When my critic heard it he said to Shamsu 'ddín that he would never in future doubt the good faith of any Ṣúfís who should assert that they attached a mystical signification to the words used in ordinary speech; and he conceived an excellent opinion of me and profited (by my writings). This was the occasion of my explaining the *Tarjumán*.'

I have now laid before the reader nearly all the available materials for a solution of this problem. How, then, does it stand with the charge of falsification brought by Dozy against Ibn al-'Arabí?

Dozy's theory seems to me untenable on the following grounds:—

[1] He wrote commentaries on two treatises by Ibn al-'Arabí (see Brockelmann, i, 443).

[2] This is the well-known historian of Aleppo.

[3] No date is mentioned in my MS. According to Ḥájjí Khalífa (ii, 277), the author finished his commentary in the second Rabí', 612 A.H. (July-August, 1215 A.D.), at Áqsaray (in Lycaonia).

(*a*) Ibn al-'Arabí does not imply, in the preface to the first recension, that the poems were composed in 598 A.H. Although he only arrived at Mecca in that year, he speaks of his acquaintance with Niẓám, the daughter of Makínu 'ddín, as something *past*, and of Makínu 'ddín himself as no longer alive.[1]

(*b*) The hypothesis that 598 A.H. was the date of composition is not required. No arguments have been advanced to show that the date given by the author, 611 A.H., is impossible or unlikely. There is nothing incredible in the statement that, while visiting the holy shrines at Mecca in this year, the author was inspired by those familiar scenes to celebrate in mystical fashion the feelings of love connected with an earlier period of his life.

(*c*) The poems themselves contain evidence that they were not composed at the date which Dozy attributes to them. The second and third verses of the thirty-second poem run as follows:—

فقلت لنفسى بعد خمسين حجّة * وقد صرت من طول التفكّر كالفرخ
يذكّرنى اكناف سلع وحاجر * ويذكر لى حال الشبيبة والشرخ

Ibn al-'Arabí was 50 years old when he wrote these verses.[2] He was born in 560 A.H., so that in 598 A.H. his age was only 38. In 611 A.H. he was 51. To say '50' instead of '51' is a small poetical licence, which needs no apology, whereas on Dozy's supposition the author must have antedated his age and post-dated his poems by considerably more than a decade in each case.

We may therefore conclude that Ibn al-'Arabí's account of the matter is correct, and that the composition of the *Tarjumán al-Ashwáq* was finished in Ramaḍán, 611 A.H. (January, 1215 A.D.). A few months afterwards the author began to write his commentary at Aleppo, for Ḥájjí Khalífa tells us that it was completed in Rabí' ath-thání of the following year (August, 1215 A.D.).

[1] This is indicated by the words رحمه الله تعالى, which follow his name.

[2] Another reference to the poet's age occurs in xxxvi, 2.

The further question, whether Ibn al-'Arabí was quite sincere when he claimed that his poems were intended to be mystical in spirit, though erotic in form, must, I think, be answered in the affirmative. Students of Oriental poetry have sometimes to ask themselves, 'Is this a love-poem disguised as a mystical ode, or a mystical ode expressed in the language of human love?' and to acknowledge that they cannot tell. Here, however, the balance is not so nicely poised that every reader may be allowed to choose the interpretation which pleases him. Some of the poems, it is true, are not distinguishable from ordinary love-songs, and as regards a great portion of the text, the attitude of the author's contemporaries, who refused to believe that it had any esoteric sense at all, was natural and intelligible; on the other hand, there are many passages which are obviously mystical and give a clue to the rest. If the sceptics lacked discernment, they deserve our gratitude for having provoked Ibn al-'Arabí to instruct them. Assuredly, without his guidance the most sympathetic readers would seldom have hit upon the hidden meanings which his fantastic ingenuity elicits from the conventional phrases of an Arabic *qaṣída.*[1] But the fact that his explanations overshoot the mark is no proof of his insincerity: he had to satisfy his critics, and it would have been difficult to convince them that the poems were mystical in spirit and intention unless he had given a precise and definite interpretation of every line and of almost every word. The necessity of entering into trivial details—an Arab is in any case apt to exaggerate details at the expense of the whole—drives the author to take refuge in far-fetched verbal analogies and causes him to descend with startling rapidity from the sublime to the

[1] The author admits that in some passages of his poems the mystical import was not clear to himself, and that various explanations were suggested to him in moments of ecstasy: كنّا قد نزعنا فى شرح هذه القطعة وغيرها منازع مختلفة فى مواضع شتّى على حسب ما يعطيه السماع فى وارد الوقت (N. 55*a*, at foot).

ridiculous. We have seen that when he published his commentary he omitted from the preface those passages relating to the beautiful and accomplished Niẓám which occur in the first recension. No doubt they had been misunderstood; it was inevitable that they should excite suspicion. To cancel them was merely to deprive his critics of a powerful weapon against which he could not defend himself effectively. For, if Niẓám was to him (and manifestly she was nothing else) a Beatrice, a type of heavenly perfection, an embodiment of Divine love and beauty, yet in the world's eyes he ran the risk of appearing as a lover who protests his devotion to an abstract ideal while openly celebrating the charms of his mistress. In the poems she is scarcely ever mentioned by name, but there are one or two particular references which I will quote here:—

'Long have I yearned for a tender maiden, endowed with prose and verse (ذات نثر ونظام), having a pulpit, eloquent,
One of the princesses from the land of Persia, from the most glorious of cities, from Iṣfahán.
She is the daughter of 'Iráq, the daughter of my Imám, and I am her opposite, a child of Yemen.'

(XX, 15–17.)

'O my two comrades, may my life-blood be the ransom of a slender girl who bestowed on me favours and bounties!
She established the harmony of union, for she is our principle of harmony (نظامنا): she is both Arab and foreign: she makes the gnostic forget.
Whenever she gazes, she draws against thee trenchant swords, and her front teeth show to thee a dazzling levin.'

(XXIX, 13–15.)

'Verily, she is an Arab girl belonging by origin to the daughters of Persia, yea, verily.
Beauty strung for her a row of fine pearly teeth, white and pure as crystal.'

(XLII, 4–5.)

Since I do not propose either to discuss the poems from a literary and artistic standpoint or to give an account of the mystical doctrines which the author has occasion to touch upon in the course of his commentary, it only remains to describe the MSS. which I have used in preparing this edition.

1. A MS. in my collection, dated 1029 A.H. It contains both the text of the poems (written with red ink) and the commentary. Inscriptions on the last page certify that it has been twice diligently collated and corrected. In referring to it I shall use the designation N.

2. A MS. in the Leiden University Library, Cod. 875 (2) Warn. (see Dozy's *Catalogue*, ii, 74). It contains only the text of the poems, with a preface, and is dated 992 A.H. In referring to it I shall use the designation L.

3. A MS. in the Leiden University Library, Cod. 641 Warn. (see Dozy's *Catalogue*, ii, 75–7). It is dated 984 A.H., and contains both text and commentary. In referring to it I shall use the designation M.

The Arabic text printed below is based on N., and the variants in LM. are noted at the foot of the page. The text, which exhibits many grammatical and metrical irregularities, is not vocalized in any of these MSS.

The commentary in N., from which my translation is made, is sometimes not so full as that in M. The latter includes a few excerpts from the *Futúḥát al-Makkiyya*. The English version of the commentary is usually very much abridged, but I have rendered the interesting and important passages nearly word for word.[1]

I shall now transcribe the text of the preface and the poems according to N. The Arabic text will be followed by an English version of the poems, with annotations based on the author's commentary.

[1] The correct title of the commentary seems to be رسالة الذخائر والأعلاق في شرح ترجمان الاشواق; it is derived from the phrase تلك الذخائر والأعلاق, which occurs in the preface (p. 12, l. 7 *infra*). The erroneous reading الأغلاق is found in most MSS., and Ḥájjí Khalífa gives the title of the commentary as فتح الذخائر والأغلاق.

THE ARABIC TEXT

بسم الله الرحمن الرحيم

الحمد لله الحسن الفعال ‘ الجميل الذى يحبّ الجمال ‘ خلق العالم فى [1] اكمل صورة وزينه ‘ وادرج فيه حكمة الغيبية [2] عند ما كوّنه ‘ واشار الى موضع السرّ منه وعيّنه ‘ [3] وفصّل للعارفين مجملة منه وبيّنه ‘ جعل ما على ارض الاجسام زينة لها ‘ فافنى العارفين فى مشاهدة تلك الزينة وجدًا ووليها ‘ وصلى الله على المتجلى اليه فى احسن صوره ‘ والمبعوث باكمل شريعة واحسن سيره ‘ محمد بن عبد الله المكلّم بالمقام العلى ‘ والمخصوص بالكمال الكلّى ‘ والتنزيل [4] الوحيى ‘ وعلى آله وصحبه [5] وسلّم ‘ اما بعد فانى لما نزلت مكة سنة ثمان وتسعين وخمسماية الفيت بها جماعة من الفضلاء ‘ وعصابة من [6] الاكابر الادباء والعلماء ‘ بين رجال خضارمة ونساء ‘ ولم ار فيهم مع فضلهم مشغولًا بنفسه ‘ مشغوفًا بالنظر فيما بين يومه وامسه ‘ مثل الشيخ العالم الامام بمقام ابراهيم عليه السلام ‘ نزيل البلد الامين ‘ مكين الدين [7] ابى شجاع زاهر بن رستم بن ابى الرجا الاصبهانى رحمه الله تعالى واخته المسنة العالمة شيخة الحجاز فخر النساء بنت رستم فاما الشيخ [8] [فسمعنا عليه كتاب ابى عيسى الترمذى فى الحديث وكثيرًا من الاجزاء فى جماعة من الفضلا‘ كان يغلب عليه الادب فكانّ جليسه فى بستان كان رحمه الله لطيف المؤانسه ‘ ظريف المجالسه ‘ يمتّع الجليس ‘ ويؤانس الانيس ‘ كان له رضى الله عنه من امره شأن يغنيه ‘ فلا يتكلم الّا فيما يعنيه‘ واما اخته فخر النساء‘ بل فخر الرجال والعلماء‘ بعثت اليها لاسمع عليها لعلوّ روايتها فقالت فنى الامل ‘ واقترب

[1] L. احسن.

[2] L. بعد.

[3] L. وفضل للعارفين بجملة.

[4] N. الروحى.

[5] L. وسلم وشرف وكرم.

[6] L. اكابر الاوليا.

[7] N. ابو.

[8] Here L. proceeds : واخته رضى الله عنهما فأخذت عن كل منهما اجازة وكان لهذا الشيخ الخ (p. 11, l. 9).

الاجل ' وشغلنى عمّا تطلبه منّى من الرواية البحث على العمل ' فكانّى بالموت قد هجم ' واقرع السنّ بالندم ' فعند ما بلغنى كلامها كتبت اليها اقول

حالى وحالك فى الرواية واحد * ما القصد الّا العلم واستعمالُهُ

فاذنت لاخيها ان يكتب لنا نيابة عنها اجازة عامّة لجميع رواياتها فكتب رضى الله عنه وعنها ذلك ودفعه لنا وكتب لنا خطه بجميع مسموعاته عليه واجازة عامّة ايضًا وكتبت اليه قصيدة عملتها فيه منها

سمعت الترمذىّ على المكين * امام الناس بالبلد الامين]

وكان لهذا الشيخ رضى الله عنه بنت عذراء ' طفلة هيفاء ' تقيّد النواظر ' وتزيّن [1]المَحاضر ' وتسرّ [2]المُحاضر ' وتحير المُناظر ' تسمّى بالنظام وتلقّب بعين الشمس والبهاء من العالمات العابدات ' [3]السائحات الزاهدات ' شيخة الحرمَيْن ' وتربية البلد الامين الاعظم بلا مَيْن ' [4]ساحرة الطرف ' عراقية الظرف ' ان اسهبت اتعبت ' وان اوجزت اعجزت ' وان افصحت اوضحت ' ان نطقت خرس قسّ بن ساعده ' وان كرمت خنس معن بن زائده ' [5][وان وفت [6]قصر السَّمَوْءَلُ خُطاه ' واعرورى ظهر الغدر وامتطاه ' ولولا النفوس الضعيفة السريعة الامراض ' السيئة الاعراض ' لاخذتُ فى شرح ما اودع الله فى خَلْقها ' من الحسن وفى خُلقها ' التى هى روضة المزن شمس بين العلماء ' بستان بين الادباء ' حقّة مختومه ' واسطة عقد منظومه ' يتيمة دهرها ' كريمة عصرها ' سابغة الكرم ' عالية الهمم ' سيدة [7]واديها ' شريفة ناديها ' مسكنها [8]جياد ' وبيتها من العين السواد ' ومن الصدر الفؤاد ' اشرقت بها تهامه ' وفتح الروض لمجاورتها اكمامه ' فنمّت اعراف ازهار المعارف ' بما تحمله من الرقايق واللطايف ' [9]عليها

[1] L. الحواظر. [2] L. الخاطر. [3] L. om.

[4] L. om. the next four words.

[5] L. om. from here to وهمّة ملك, p. 12, l. 1.

[6] N. قصرت شمول خطاه. [7] N. والديها.

[8] See the *Marâsid* under اجياد. [9] N. علمها.

مسحة مَلَك ، وهمّة مَلِك ،] فراعينا فى صحبتها كرم ذاتها مع ما
[1]انضاف الى ذلك من صحبة العمّة والوالد فقلّدناها من نظمنا فى
هذا الكتاب احسن القلايد بلسان نسيب رايق ، وعبارات الغزل
اللايق ، ولم ابلغ بذلك بعض ما تجده النفس ، [2]ويثيره الانس ،
من كريم ودّها ، وقديم عهدها ، [3][ولطافة معناها ، وطهارة مغناها ، اذ
هى السؤل والمأمول ، والعذراء البتول ، ولكن نظمنا فيها بعض خاطر
الاشتياق ، من تلك الذخاير والاعلاق ، فاعربتُ عن نفس تواقه ،
ونبّهت على ما عندنا من العلاقه ، اهتمامًا بالعهد القديم ، وايثارًا
بالمجلس الكريم ،] فكل اسم اذكره فى هذا الجزء فعنها اكنى ، وكل
دار اندبها فدارها اعنى ، ولم ازل فيما نظمته [4]فى هذا الجزء من
الايماء الى الواردات الالاهيه ، والتنزّلات الروحانيه ، والمناسبات
العلويه ، [5]جريًا على [6]طريقتنا المُثلى ، [7]فان الآخرة خير من الأولَى ،
ولعلمها رضى الله عنها [8]لما اليه اشير ، ولا ينبئُك مثل خبير ، والله
يعصم قارئ هذا الجزء وساير الديوان من سبق خاطره الى ما لا يليق
بالنفوس الابيه ، والهمم العليه ، المتعلقة بالامور السماويه ، آمين
بعزته لا ربّ غيره والله يقول الحق وهو يهدى السبيل ، [9][فاستخرت
الله تعالى وقيّدت فى هذه الاوراق ما نظمته من الابيات الغزليه بمكة
شرفها الله تعالى وعظّمها فى حال اعتمارى فى رجب وشعبان ورمضان
اشير بها الى معارف ربانيه ، واسرار روحانيه ، وعلوم عقليه ، وتنبيهات
شرعيه ، وجعلت العبارة عن ذلك بلسان الغزل والنسيب لتعشّق
النفوس لهذه العبارات فتتوفر الدواعى على الاصغاء اليها ، وقد نبّهت
بالمقصد فى ذلك بابيات] [10]وهى هذه

[1] L. يضاف.

[2] L. ويثير.

[3] L. om. from here to وايثارًا بالمجلس الكريم, l. 9.

[4] L. من.

[5] L. جار.

[6] Kor. 20, 66.

[7] Kor. 93, 4.

[8] So LN., but the sense seems to require بما.

[9] L. om. from here to بابيات, last line.

[10] L. وهذه اول الابيات.

١ كُلَّما أَذْكُرُهُ من طَلَلٍ * او رُبوعٍ او [1]مَغانٍ كُلَّما

٢ وكذا إن قلتُ ها او قلتُ يا * [2]وأَلا إن جآء فيه او أَما

٣ وكذا إن قلتُ [3]هى او قلتُ [4]هو * او هُمو او هُنَّ جَمْعًا او هُما

٤ وكذا إن قلتُ قد أَنْجَدَ بى * قَدَرٌ فى شِعْرنا او أَتْهَما

٥ وكذا [5]السُّحْبُ اذا قلتُ بَكَتْ * وكذا الزَّهْرُ اذا ما ٱبْتَسَما

٦ [6]او أُنادى بحُداةٍ يَمَّموا * بانةَ الحاجِرِ او وُرْقَ الحِما

٧ او بُدورٍ فى خُدورٍ أَفَلَتْ * او شُموسٍ او بناتٍ [7]نُجُما

٨ او بُروقٍ او رُعودٍ او صَبًا * او رِياحٍ او جَنوبٍ او [8]شَمَا

٩ او طريقٍ او عقيقٍ او نَقًا * [9]او جِبالٍ او خِيالٍ او [10]رِما

١٠ او خليلٍ او رحيلٍ او رُبًا * او رِياضٍ او غِياضٍ او حِمى

١١ او نِساءٍ كاعباتٍ نُهَّدٍ * طالعاتٍ [11]او شُموسٍ او دُمَى

١٢ كُلَّما أَذْكُرُهُ مِمّا جرى * ذِكْرُهُ او [12]مِثْلُهُ إن [13]تَفْهَما

١٣ منه أَسْرارٌ وأنوارٌ جِلا * او عُلًى جآء بها [14]رَكْبُ السَّما

١٤ لِفُؤادى او فُؤادِ مَنْ له * مِثْلُ ما لى من شُروطِ العُلَما

١٥ صِفَةٌ قُدْسِيَّةٌ عُلْوِيَّةٌ * أَعْلَمَتْ أَنَّ لِصِدْقى قَدَما

١٦ فٱصْرِفِ الخاطِرَ عن ظاهِرِها * [15]وٱطْلُبِ الباطِنَ حتّى تَعْلَما

[1] M. مقام.

[2] M. فاشارة اليها واما.

[3] M. هو. [4] M. هى. [5] M. الزهر.

[6] This verse is the fourth in L.

[7] L. بخما ; M. او شموس او بنات او هلال نجما.

[8] For شمال.

[9] L. او خيال او جبال ; M. او خيام او جبال.

[10] For رمال. [11] LM. كشموس.

[12] M. شبهه ; so N. in marg. [13] M. نفهما.

[14] L. رب السما. [15] L. واترك.

فمن ذلك حكاية جرت لى فى الطواف كنت اطوف ذات ليلة بالبيت فطاب وقتى وهزّنى حال كنت اعرفه فخرجت من البلاط من اجل الناس وطفت على الرمل فحضرتنى ابيات فانشدتها أسمع بها نفسى ومن يلينى لو كان هناك احد

لَيْتَ شِعْرِى هل دَرَوْا * اىَّ قَلْبٍ مَلَكُوا
وفُؤادِى لَوْ دَرَى * اىَّ شِعْبٍ سَلَكُوا
أَتُراهُمْ سَلِموا * أَمْ تَراهم هَلَكُوا
حارَ أَرْبابُ الهَوَى * فى الهَوَى وارْتَبَكُوا

قال فلم اشعر الّا بضربة بين كتفىّ بكفّ أَلْيَنَ من الخزّ فالتفتُّ فاذا انا بجارية من بنات الروم لم ار احسن منها وجهًا ولا اعذب منها منطقًا ولا ارقّ حاشيةً ولا الطف معنًى ولا ادقّ اشارةً ولا اظرف محاورةً منها فاقت اهل زمانها ظرفًا وادبًا وجمالًا ومعرفةً فقالت يا سيّدى كيف قلت فقلت

ليت شعرى هل دروا * اىّ قلب ملكوا

فقالت عجبًا منك وانت عارفُ زمانك تقول مثل هذا القول أليس كل مملوك معروف وهل يصحّ الملك الّا بعد المعرفة وتمنّى الشعور يؤذن بعدمها والطريق لسان صدق فكيف يتجوّز مثلك قل يا سيّدى ما قلت بعده فقلت

وفؤادى لو درى * اىّ شعب سلكوا

فقالت يا سيّدى الشعب الذى بين الشغاف والفؤاد وهو المانع له من المعرفة فكيف يتمنى مثلك ما لا يمكن الوصول اليه والطريق لسان صدق فكيف يتجوّز مثلك يا سيّدى ما ذا قلت بعده فقلت

اتراهم سلموا * ام تراهم هلكوا

فقالت اما هم فسلموا ولكن عنك ينبغى ان تسأل نفسك هل سلمت ام هلكت يا سيّدى فما ذا قلت بعده فقلت

حار ارباب الهوى * فى الهوى وارتبكوا

فصاحت وقالت وا عجبا كيف ينبغى للمشغوف فضلةٌ يحار بها والهوى شأنه التعميم يخدّر الحواسّ ويُذهب العقول ويُدهش الخواطر ويذهب بصاحبه فى الذاهبين فاين الحيرة ومَنْ هنا باقٍ فيحارَ والطريق لسان صدق والتجوّز من مثلك غير لايق فقلت يا بنت الخالة ما اسمك قالت قُرّة العين [1]فقلتُ لى ثمّ سلّمت وانصرفت ثمّ انّى عرفتها بعد ذلك وعاشرتها فرايت عندها من لطايف المعرفة ما لا يصفه واصف شرح الابيات الاربع

I

١ لَيْتَ شِعْرِى هَلْ دَرَوْا * أَىَّ قَلْبٍ مَلَكوا
٢ وفُؤادِى لَوْ دَرَى * أَىَّ شِعْبٍ سَلَكوا
٣ أَتَراهُمْ سَلِموا * أَمْ تَراهُمْ هَلَكوا
٤ حارَ أَرْبابُ ٱلْهَوَى * فى ٱلْهَوَى وٱرْتَبَكوا

٣ L. او for ام . ٤ L. حارت ; this is the original reading of N., but the final ت has been erased by a corrector.

II

١ ما رَحَّلوا يَوْمَ بانوا ٱلْبُزَّلَ ٱلْعِيسا * إِلّا وقد حَمَلوا فيها ٱلطَّواوِيسا
٢ مِنْ كُلِّ فاتِكَةِ ٱلْأَلْحاظِ مالِكَةٍ * تَخالُها فَوْقَ عَرْشِ ٱلدُّرِّ بِلْقِيسا
٣ إِذا تَمَشَّتْ على صَرْحِ ٱلزُّجاجِ تَرَى * شَمْسًا على فَلَكٍ فى حِجْرِ إِدْرِيسا
٤ يُحْيِى إِذا قَتَلَتْ بِٱللَّحْظِ مَنْطِقُها * كَأَنَّها عند ما تُحْيِى بِه عِيسَى
٥ تَوْراتُها لَوْحُ ساقَيْها سَنًا وأَنا * أَتْلو وأَدْرُسُها كَأَنَّنى مُوسَى
٦ أُسْقُفَّةٌ مِنْ بَناتِ ٱلرُّومِ عاطِلَةٌ * تَرَى عَلَيْها مِنَ ٱلْأَنْوارِ نامُوسا
٧ وَحْشِيَّةٌ ما بِها أُنْسٌ قَدِ ٱتَّخَذَتْ * فى بَيْتِ خَلْوَتِها لِلذِّكْرِ ناوُوسا
٨ قد أَعْجَزَتْ كُلَّ عَلّامٍ بِمِلَّتِنا * وداوُدِيًّا وحَبْرًا ثُمَّ قِسِّيسا
٩ إِنْ أَوْمَأَتْ تَطْلُبُ ٱلْإِنْجِيلَ تَحْسَبُنا * أَقِسَّةً أَوْ بَطارِيقًا شَمامِيسا

١ L. ساروا for بانوا . ٤ N. اذا تُحيى . ٦ L. بنات الترك .

[1] M. قلت .

١٠ شَبَّبْتُ أَجْنادَ صَبْرِى يَوْمَ بَيْنِهِمُ * عَلَى ٱلطَّرِيقِ كَرادِيسًا كَرادِيسا

١١ سَأَلْتُ إِذْ بَلَغَتْ نَفْسِى تَراقِيَها * ذاكَ ٱلْجَمالَ وَذاكَ ٱللُّطْفَ تَنْفِيسا

١٢ فَأَسْلَمَتْ وَوَقانا ٱللّٰهُ شِرَّتَها * وَزَحْزَحَ ٱلْمَلِكُ ٱلْمَنْصُورُ إِبْلِيسا

١٣ نادَيْتُ إِذْ رَحَلَتْ لِلْبَيْنِ ناقَتُها * يا حادِىَ ٱلْعِيسِ لا تَحْدُو بِها العِيسا

١٠ L. اجياد. ١١ L. ان for اذ. ١٣ This verse is the tenth in L. and M.

III

١ خَلِيلَيَّ عُوجا بِالكَثِيبِ وَعَرِّجا * على لَعْلَعٍ وَٱطْلُبْ مِياهَ يَلَمْلَمِ

٢ فَإِنَّ بِها مَنْ قد عَلِمْتَ وَمَنْ لَهُمْ * صِيامِى وَحَجِّى وَٱعْتِمارِى وَمَوْسِمِى

٣ فَلا أَنْسَ يَوْمًا بِٱلْمُحَصَّبِ مِنْ مِنًى * وَبِٱلْمَنْحَرِ ٱلْأَعْلَى أُمُورًا وَزَمْزَمِ

٤ مُحَصَّبُهُمْ قَلْبِى لِرَمْىِ جِمارِهِمْ * وَمَنْحَرُهُمْ نَفْسِى وَمَشْرَبُهُمْ دَمِى

٥ فيا حادِىَ ٱلْأَجْمالِ إِنْ جِئْتَ حاجِرًا * فَقِفْ بِٱلْمَطايا ساعَةً ثُمَّ سَلِّمِ

٦ وَنادِ ٱلْقِبابَ ٱلْحُمْرَ مِنْ جانِبِ ٱلْحِمَى * تَحِيَّةَ مُشْتاقٍ إِلَيْكُمْ مُتَيَّمِ

٧ فَإِنْ سَلَّمُوا فَٱهْدِ ٱلسَّلامَ مَعَ ٱلصَّبا * وَإِنْ سَكَتُوا فَٱرْحَلْ بِها وَتَقَدَّمِ

٨ إِلَى نَهْرِ عِيسَى حَيْثُ حَلَّ رِكابُهُمْ * وَحَيْثُ ٱلْخِيامُ ٱلْبِيضُ مِنْ جانِبِ ٱلْفَمِ

٩ وَنادِ بِدَعْدٍ وَٱلرَّبابِ وَزَيْنَبٍ * وَهِنْدٍ وَسَلْمَى ثُمَّ لُبْنَى وَزَمْزَمِ

١٠ وَسَلْهُنَّ هَلْ بِٱلْحِلَّةِ ٱلْغادَةُ ٱلَّتِى * تُرِيكَ سَنا ٱلْبَيْضاءِ عِنْدَ ٱلتَّبَسُّمِ

١ L. واقصد. ٢ L. عهدت. ٣ L. فلم انس. ٥ L. الاضعان [sic]. ٦ L. البيض ; L. اليهم. ٨ LM. حلت. ٩ N. in marg. وفرتنا for وزينب. ١٠ N. بالحلّة.

IV

١ سَلامٌ عَلَى سَلْمَى وَمَنْ حَلَّ بِٱلْحِمَى * وَحَقٌّ لِمِثْلِى رِقَّةً أَنْ يُسَلِّما

٢ وَما ذا عَلَيْها لَوْ تَرُدُّ تَحِيَّةً * عَلَيْنا وَلٰكِنْ لا ٱحْتِكامَ عَلَى الدُّمَى

٣ سَرَوْا وَظَلامُ ٱللَّيْلِ أَرْخَى سُدُولَهُ * فَقُلْتُ لَها صَبًّا غَرِيبًا مُتَيَّما

١ L. سلامى. ٢ M. ان تردّ.

٤ أَحاطَتْ بِهِ ٱلْأَشواقُ شَوْقًا وأُرصِدَتْ * لَهُ راشِقاتُ ٱلنَّبْلِ أَيانَ يَمَّما

٥ فأَبْدَتْ ثَناياها وأَوْمَضَ بارِقٌ * فلَمْ أَدْرِ مَنْ شَقَّ ٱلحَنادِسَ مِنْهُما

٦ وقالَتْ أَما يَكْفِيهِ أَنّى بِقَلْبِهِ * يُشاهِدُنى فى كُلِّ وَقْتٍ أَما أَما

٤ L. صورا for شوقًا ; M. سورا supp. above.

V

١ أَنْجَدَ ٱلشَّوْقُ وأَتْهَمَ ٱلغَرامْ * فأَنا ما بَيْنَ نَجْدٍ وتِهامْ

٢ وهُما ضِدّانِ لَنْ يَجْتَمِعا * فشَتاتى ما لَهُ ٱلدَّهْرَ نِظامْ

٣ ما صَنيعى ما ٱحْتِيالى دُلَّنى * يا عَذولى لا تَرُعْنى بِٱلمَلامْ

٤ زَفَراتٌ قَدْ تَعالَتْ صُعُدًا * ودُموعٌ فَوْقَ خَدّى سِجامْ

٥ حَنَّتِ ٱلعِيسُ إِلَى أَوْطانِها * مِنْ وَجَى ٱلسَّيْرِ حَنِينَ ٱلمُسْتَهامْ

٦ ما حَياتى بَعْدَهُمْ إِلّا ٱلفَنا * فعَلَيْها وعَلَى ٱلصَّبْرِ ٱلسَّلامْ

٢ L. لم for لن.

VI

١ بانَ ٱلعَزآءُ وبانَ ٱلصَّبْرُ إِذْ بانوا * بانوا وهُمْ فى سُوَيْدِ ٱلقَلْبِ سُكّانُ

٢ سَأَلْتُهُمْ عَنْ مَقِيلِ ٱلرَّكْبِ قِيلَ لَنا * مَقيلُهُمْ حَيْثُ فاحَ ٱلشِّيحُ وٱلبانُ

٣ فقُلْتُ لِلرِّيحِ سِيرى وٱلْحَقِى بِهِمِ * فإِنَّهُمْ عِنْدَ ظِلِّ ٱلأَيْكِ قُطّانُ

٤ وبَلِّغِيهِمْ سَلامًا مِنْ أَخى شَجَنٍ * فى قَلْبِهِ مِنْ فِراقِ ٱلقَوْمِ أَشْجانُ

١ L. سويدا ; M. سواد.

VII

١ وزاحَمَنى عِنْدَ ٱسْتِلامى أَوانِسٌ * أَتَيْنَ إِلَى ٱلتَّطْوافِ مُعْتَجِراتِ

٢ حَسَرْنَ عَنَ ٱنْوارِ ٱلشُّموسِ وقُلْنَ لى * تَوَرَّعْ فمَوْتُ ٱلنَّفْسِ فى ٱللَّحَظاتِ

٣ فكَمْ قَدْ قَتَلْنا بِٱلمُحَصَّبِ مِنْ مِنًى * نُفُوسًا أَبِيّاتٍ لَدَى ٱلجَمَراتِ

٤ وفى سَرْحَةِ ٱلوادى وأَعْلامِ رامَةٍ * وجَمْعٍ وعِنْدَ ٱلنَّفْرِ مِن عَرَفاتِ

٥ أَلَمْ تَرَ أَنَّ ٱلحُسْنَ يَسْلُبُ مَنْ لَهُ * عَفافٌ فيُدْعَى سالِبَ ٱلحَسَناتِ

٢ L. عن امثال الشموس . ٥ M. الم تدر .

٦ فَمَوْعِدُنا بَعْدَ ٱلطَّوافِ بِزَمْزَمٍ * لَدَى ٱلْقُبَّةِ ٱلْوُسْطَى لَدَى ٱلصَّخَراتِ
٧ هُنالِكَ مَنْ قَدْ شَفَّهُ ٱلْوَجْدُ يَشْتَفِي * بِما شاقَهُ مِنْ نِسْوَةٍ عَطِراتِ
٨ إِذا خِفْنَ أَسْدَلْنَ ٱلشُّعُورَ فَهُنَّ مِنْ * غَدايِرِها فِى أَلْحُفِ ٱلظُّلُماتِ

٦ N. عند الطواف. ٧ LM. بما شاءه. ٨ L. الحبرات.

VIII

١ دَرَسَتْ رُبُوعُهُمُ وَإِنَّ هَواهُمُ * أَبَدًا جَدِيدٌ بِٱلْحَشَى لا يَدْرُسُ
٢ هٰذِى طُلُولُهُمُ وَهٰذِى ٱلْأَدْمُعُ * وَلِذِكْرِهِمْ أَبَدًا تَذُوبُ ٱلْأَنْفُسُ
٣ نادَيْتُ خَلْفَ رِكابِهِمْ مِنْ حُبِّهِمْ * يا مَنْ غِناهُ ٱلْحُسْنُ ها أَنا مُفْلِسُ
٤ مَرَّغْتُ خَدِّى رِقَّةً وَصَبابَةً * فَبِحَقِّ حَقِّ هَواكُمُ لا تُؤْيِسُوا
٥ مَنْ ظَلَّ فِى عَبَراتِهِ غَرِقًا وَفِى * نارِ ٱلْأَسَى حَرِقًا وَلا مُتَنَفَّسُ
٦ يا مُوقِدَ ٱلنّارِ ٱلرُّوَيْدا هٰذِهِ * نارُ ٱلصَّبابَةِ شَأْنُكُمْ فَلْتَقْبِسُوا

٢ L. ادمعى. ٥ L. يتنفس.

IX

١ لَمَعَتْ لَنا بِٱلْأَبْرَقَيْنِ بُرُوقُ * قَصَفَتْ لَها بَيْنَ ٱلضُّلُوعِ رُعُودُ
٢ وَهَمَتْ سَحايِبُها بِكُلِّ خَمِيلَةٍ * وَبِكُلِّ مَيّادٍ عَلَيْكَ يَمِيدُ
٣ فَجَرَتْ مَذانِبُها وَفاحَ نَسِيمُها * وَهَفَتْ مُطَوَّقَةٌ وَأَوْرَقَ عُودُ
٤ نَصَبُوا ٱلْقِبابَ ٱلْحُمْرَ بَيْنَ جَداوِلٍ * مِثْلِ ٱلْأَساوِدِ بَيْنَهُنَّ قُعُودُ
٥ بِيضٌ أَوانِسُ كَٱلشُّمُوسِ طَوالِعٌ * عِينٌ كَرِيماتٌ عَقايِلُ غِيدُ

١ M. فصفت. ٣ N. مداينها; in marg. منابتها. ٥ L. رود for غيد.

X[1]

١ قالَتْ عَجِبْتُ لِصَبٍّ مِنْ مَحاسِنِهِ * يَخْتالُ ما بَيْنَ أَزْهارٍ بِبُسْتانِ
٢ فَقُلْتُ لا تَعْجَبِى مِمّا تَرَيْنَ فَقَدْ * أَبْصَرْتِ نَفْسَكِ فِى مِرْآةِ إِنْسانِ

[1] L. omits this poem.

XI

١ أَلا يا حَماماتِ ٱلْأَراكَةِ وَٱلْبانِ * تَرَفَّقْنَ لا تُضْعِفْنَ بِٱلشَّجْوِ أَشْجانى

٢ تَرَفَّقْنَ لا تُظْهِرْنَ بِٱلنَّوْحِ وَٱلْبُكا * خَفِىَّ صَباباتى وَمَكْنُونَ أَحْزانى

٣ أُطارِحُها عِنْدَ ٱلْأَصِيلِ وَبِٱلضُّحَى * بِحَنَّةِ مُشْتاقٍ وَأَنَّةِ هَيْمانِ

٤ تَناوَحَتِ ٱلْأَرْواحُ فى غَيْضَةِ ٱلْغَضَى * فَمالَتْ بِأَفْنانٍ عَلَىَّ فَأَفْنانى

٥ وَجاءَتْ مِنَ ٱلشَّوْقِ ٱلْمُبَرِّحِ وَٱلْجَوَى * وَمِنْ طُرَفِ ٱلْبَلْوَى إِلَىَّ بِأَفْنانِ

٦ فَمَنْ لى بِجَمْعٍ وَٱلْمُحَصَّبِ مِن مِنًى * وَمَنْ لى بِذاتِ ٱلْأَثْلِ مَنْ لى بِنَعْمانِ

٧ تَطُوفُ بِقَلْبى ساعَةً بَعْدَ ساعَةٍ * لِوَجْدٍ وَتَبْرِيحٍ وَتَلْثِمُ أَرْكانى

٨ كَما طافَ خَيْرُ ٱلْخَلْقِ بِٱلْكَعْبَةِ ٱلَّتى * يَقُولُ دَلِيلُ ٱلْعَقْلِ فيها بِنُقْصانِ

٩ وَقَبَّلَ أَحْجارًا بِها وَهُوَ ناطِقٌ * وَأَيْنَ مَقامُ ٱلْبَيْتِ مِن قَدْرِ إِنْسانِ

١٠ وَكَمْ عَهِدَتْ أَن لا تَحُولَ وَأَقْسَمَتْ * وَلَيْسَ لِمَخْضُوبٍ وَفاءٌ بِأَيْمانِ

١١ وَمِنْ أَعْجَبِ ٱلْأَشْياءِ ظَبْىٌ مُبَرْقَعٌ * يُشِيرُ بِعُنّابٍ وَيُومِى بِأَجْفانِ

١٢ وَمَرْعاهُ ما بَيْنَ ٱلتَّرائِبِ وَٱلْحَشَى * وَيا عَجَبًا مِن رَوْضَةٍ وَسْطَ نِيرانِ

١٣ لَقَدْ صارَ قَلْبى قابِلًا كُلَّ صُورَةٍ * فَمَرْعًى لِغِزْلانٍ وَدَيْرٌ لِرُهْبانِ

١٤ وَبَيْتٌ لِأَوْثانٍ وَكَعْبَةُ طائِفٍ * وَأَلْواحُ تَوْراتٍ وَمُصْحَفُ قُرْآنِ

١٥ أَدِينُ بِدِينِ ٱلْحُبِّ أَنَّى تَوَجَّهَتْ * رَكائِبُهُ فَٱلدِّينُ دِينى وَإِيمانى

١٦ لَنا أُسْوَةٌ فى بِشْرِ هِنْدٍ وَأُخْتِها * وَقَيْسٍ وَلَيْلَى ثُمَّ مَىٍّ وَغَيْلانِ

٢ Here begins a lacuna in M. extending to the tenth verse of the twenty-second poem. ٤ L. ومالت . ٦ L. بالمحصّب . ٧ L. بوجد . ٨ N. بنقصانى . ١٠ N. in marg. تخون . ١٦ L. وقيس ولبنى ; · L. ميا .

XII

١ بِذى سَلَمٍ وَٱلدَّيْرِ مِن حاضِرِ ٱلْحِمَى * ظِباءٌ تُرِيكَ ٱلشَّمْسَ فى صُوَرِ ٱلدُّمَى

٢ فَأَرْقُبُ أَفْلاكًا وَأَخْدُمُ بِيعَةً * وَأَحْرُسُ رَوْضًا بِٱلرَّبِيعِ مُنَمْنَما

٣ فَوَقْتًا أُسَمَّى راعِىَ ٱلظَّبْىِ بِٱلْفَلا * وَوَقْتًا أُسَمَّى راهِبًا وَمُنَجِّما

٤ تَثَلَّثَ مَحْبُوبِى وقد كان واحِدًا * كما صُيِّرَ ٱلأَقْنامُ بِٱلذاتِ أَقْنُما

٥ فلا تُنْكِرَنْ يا صاحِ قَوْلِى غَزالَةٌ * تُضِىءُ لِغِزْلانٍ يَطُفْنَ على ٱلدُّمَى

٦ فلِلظَّبْيِ أَجْيادًا ولِلشَّمْسِ أَوْجُهًا * ولِلدُّمْيَةِ ٱلبَيْضاءِ صَدْرًا ومِعْصَما

٧ كما قد أَعَرْنا لِلْغُصُونِ مَلابِسًا * ولِلرَّوْضِ أَخْلاقًا ولِلْبَرْقِ مَبْسِما

٤ L. صيروا. ٦ L. اجياد.

XIII

١ ناحَتْ مُطَوَّقَةٌ فحَنَّ حَزِينُ * وشَجاهُ تَرْجِيعٌ لها وحَنِينُ

٢ جَرَتِ ٱلدُّموعُ مِنَ ٱلعُيُونِ تَفَجُّعًا * لِحَنِينِها فكأَنَّهُنَّ عُيُونُ

٣ طارَحْتُها ثُكْلًا بِفَقْدِ وَحِيدِها * وٱلثُّكْلُ مِن فَقْدِ ٱلوَحِيدِ يَكُونُ

٤ طارَحْتُها وٱلشَّجْوُ يَمْشِى بَيْنَنا * ما إِنْ تَبِينُ وإِنَّنِى لَأُبِينُ

٥ بِى لاعِجٌ من حُبِّ رَمْلَةِ عالِجٍ * حَيْثُ ٱلخِيامُ بِها وحَيْثُ ٱلعِينُ

٦ من كُلِّ فاتِكَةِ ٱللِّحاظِ مَرِيضَةٍ * أَجْفانُها لِظُبَى ٱللِّحاظِ جُفُونُ

٧ ما زِلْتُ أُجْرِعُ دَمْعَتِى من غِلَّتِى * أُخْفِى ٱلهَوَى عن عاذِلِى وأَصُونُ

٨ حتّى اذا صاحَ ٱلغُرابُ بِبَيْنِهِمْ * فَضَحَ ٱلفِراقُ صَبابَةَ ٱلمَحْزُونِ

٩ وَصَلُوا ٱلسُّرَى قَطَعُوا ٱلبُرَى فلِعِيسِهِمْ * تَحْتَ ٱلمَحامِلِ رَنَّةٌ وأَنِينُ

١٠ عايَنْتُ أَسْبابَ ٱلمَنِيَّةِ عند ما * أَرْخَوْا أَزِمَّتَها وشُدَّ وَضِينُ

١١ إِنَّ ٱلفِراقَ مَعَ ٱلغَرامِ لَقاتِلٌ * صَعْبُ ٱلغَرامِ مَعَ ٱللِّقاءِ يَهُونُ

١٢ ما لِى عَذُولٌ فى هَواها إِنَّها * مَعْشُوقَةٌ حَسْناءُ حَيْثُ تَكُونُ

١ L. لها وانين. ٣ L. ثكلى.

XIV

١ رَأَى ٱلبَرْقَ شَرْقِيًّا فحَنَّ إلى ٱلشَّرْقِ * ولو لاحَ غَرْبِيًّا لَحَنَّ إلى ٱلغَرْبِ

٢ فإِنَّ غَرامِى بِٱلبُرَيْقِ ولَمْحِهِ * ولَيْسَ غَرامِى بِٱلأَماكِنِ وٱلتُّرْبِ

٣ رَوَتْ لى ٱلصَّبا عَنْهُمْ حديثًا مُعَنْعَنًا * عنِ ٱلْبَثِّ عن وَجْدى عن ٱلْحُزْنِ عن كَرْبى
٤ عنِ ٱلسُّكْرِ عن عَقْلى عن ٱلشَّوْقِ عن جَوًى * عنِ ٱلدَّمْعِ عن جَفْنى عنِ ٱلنارِ عن قَلْبى
٥ بِأَنَّ ٱلَّذى تَهْواهُ بَيْنَ ضُلوعِكُمْ * تُقَلِّبُهُ ٱلْأَنْفاسُ جَنْبًا إلى جَنْبِ
٦ فَقُلْتُ لَها بَلِّغْ إِلَيْهِ بِأَنَّهُ * هُوَ ٱلْمُوقِدُ ٱلنّارَ ٱلَّتى داخِلَ ٱلْقَلْبِ
٧ فإِنْ كان إِطْفاءٌ فَوَصْلٌ مُخَلَّدٌ * وإِنْ كان إِحْراقٌ فلا ذَنْبَ لِلصَّبِّ

٧ L. اطفاها.

XV

١ غادَرونى بِٱلْأُثَيْلِ وَٱلنَّقا * أَسْكُبُ ٱلدَّمْعَ وَأَشْكو ٱلْحَرَقا
٢ بِأَبى مَنْ ذُبْتُ فيه كَمَدًا * بِأَبى مَنْ مِتُّ فيه فَرَقا
٣ حُمْرَةُ ٱلْخَجْلَةِ فى وَجْنَتِهِ * وَضَحُ ٱلصُّبْحِ يُناغِى ٱلشَّفَقا
٤ قَوَّضَ ٱلصَّبْرُ وَطَنَّبَ ٱلْأَسَى * وأَنا ما بَيْنَ هٰذَيْنِ لِقا
٥ مَنْ لِيَبْقَى مَنْ لِوَجْدى دُلَّنى * مَنْ لِحُزْنى مَنْ لِصَبٍّ عَشِقا
٦ كُلَّما صُنْتُ تَباريحَ ٱلْهَوَى * فَضَحَ ٱلدَّمْعُ ٱلْجَوَى وَٱلْأَرَقا
٧ فإِذا قُلْتُ هَبُونى نَظْرَةً * قيلَ ما تَمْنَعُ إِلّا شَفَقا
٨ ما عَسَى يُغْنيكَ مِنْهُمْ نَظْرَةٌ * هِىَ إِلّا لَمْحُ بَرْقٍ بَرَقا
٩ لَسْتُ أَنْسَى إِذْ حَدا ٱلْحادى بِهِمْ * يَطْلُبُ ٱلْبَيْنَ وَيَبْغِى ٱلْأَبْرَقا
١٠ نَعَقَتْ أَغْرِبَةُ ٱلْبَيْنِ بِهِمْ * لا رَعَى ٱللّٰهُ غُرابًا نَعَقا
١١ ما غُرابُ ٱلْبَيْنِ إِلّا جَمَلٌ * سارَ بِٱلْأَحْبابِ نَصًّا عَنَقا

٧ L. هبوا لى. ٨ L. تغنيك. ٩ L. نطلب ; L. ونبغى. ١٠ L. نغقت.

XVI

١ حَمَلْنَ على ٱلْيَعْمَلاتِ ٱلْخُدورا * وأَوْدَعْنَ فيها ٱلدُّمَى وَٱلْبُدورا
٢ وواعَدْنَ قَلْبِى أَنْ يَرْجِعوا * وهَلْ تَعِدُ ٱلْخُودُ إِلّا غُرورا
٣ وحَيَّتْ بِعُنّابِها لِلْوَداعِ * فأَذْرَتْ دُموعًا تَهيجُ ٱلسَّعيرا

٢ L. واودعن.

٤ فلمّا تولّت وقد يمّمت * تريد الخورنق ثمّ السّديرا

٥ دعوت ثبورًا على إثرهم * فردّت وقالت أتدعو ثبورا

٦ فلا تدعونّ بها واحدًا * ولكنّما ادعُ ثبورًا كثيرا

٧ ألا يا حمام الأراك قليلًا * فما زادك البين إلّا هديرا

٨ ونوحك يا أيّها ذا الحمام * يثير المشوق يهيج الغيورا

٩ يذيب الفؤاد يذود الرّقاد * يضاعف أشواقنا والزّفيرا

١٠ يحوم الحمام لنوح الحمام * فنسأل منه البقاء يسيرا

١١ عسى نفحة من صبا حاجر * تسوق إلينا سحابًا مطيرا

١٢ تروّي بها أنفسًا قد ظمين * فما ازداد سحبك إلّا نفورا

١٣ فيا راعي النّجم كن لي نديمًا * ويا ساهر البرق كن لي سميرا

١٤ ويا راقد اللّيل هنّيته * فقبل الممات عمرت القبورا

١٥ فلو كنت تهوى الفتاة العروب * لنلت النّعيم بها والسّرورا

١٦ تعاطي الحسان خمور الخمار * تناجي الشّموس تناغي البدورا

٨ L. تثير ; L. تزيد الغيورا . ٩ L. omits this verse.

١٥ N. الفتاة الكعوب, but العروب in marg. ; LM. العروبا .

XVII

١ يا حادي العيس لا تعجل بها وقفًا * فإنّني زمن في إثرها غادي

٢ قف بالمطيّ وشمّر من أزمّتها * بالله بالوجد بالتّبريح يا حادي

٣ نفسي تريد ولكن لا تساعدها * رجلي فمن لي بإشفاق وإسعاد

٤ ما يفعل الصانع النّحرير في شغل * آلاته آذنت فيه بإفساد

٥ عرّج ففي أيمن الوادي خيامهم * لله درّك ما تحويه يا وادي

٦ جمّعت قومًا هم نفسي وهم نفسي * وهم سواد سويدا خلب أكبادي

٧ لا درّ درّ الهوى إن لم أمت كمدًا * بحاجر او بسلع او بأجياد

٢ LM. بالمطايا .

XVIII

١ قِفْ بِٱلمَنازِلِ وَٱنْدُبِ ٱلأَطْلالا * وَسَلِ الرُّبُوعَ الدّارِساتِ سُؤالا

٢ أَيْنَ ٱلأَحِبَّةُ أَيْنَ سارَتْ عِيسُهُمْ * هاتيكَ تَقْطَعُ فى ٱلْبَيابِ آلالا

٣ مِثْلَ ٱلحَدايِقِ فى السَّرابِ تَراهُمُ * ٱلآلُ يُعْظِمُ فى ٱلعُيُونِ آلالا

٤ سارُوا يُرِيدُونَ ٱلعُذَيْبَ لِيَشْرَبُوا * مآءً بِهِ مِثْلَ ٱلحَياةِ زُلالا

٥ فَقَفَوْتُ أَسْأَلُ عَنْهُمُ رِيحَ ٱلصَّبا * هَلْ خَيَّمُوا او إِسْتَظَلُّوا ٱلضّالا

٦ قالَتْ تَرَكْتُ على زَرُودَ قِبابَهُمْ * وَٱلعِيسُ تَشْكُو مِن سُراها كَلالا

٧ قَدْ أَسْدَلُوا فَوْقَ ٱلقِبابِ مَصاوِنًا * يَسْتُرْنَ مِن حَرِّ ٱلهَجِيرِ جَمالا

٨ فَٱنْهَضْ إِلَيْهِمْ طالِبًا آثارَهُمْ * وَٱرْقِلْ بِعِيسِكَ نَحْوَهُمْ إِرْقالا

٩ فَإِذا وَقَفْتَ على مَعالِمِ حاجِرٍ * وَقَطَعْتَ أَغْوارًا بِها وَجِبالا

١٠ قَرِبَتْ مَنازِلُهُمْ ولاحَتْ نارُهُمْ * نارٌ قَدَ ٱشْعَلَتِ ٱلْهَوَى إِشْعالا

١١ فَأَنِخْ بِها لا يُرْهِبَنَّكَ أُسْدُها * فَٱلِاشْتِياقُ يُرِيكَها أَشْبالا

٢ L. فى الفياف . ٥ L. هل استضلّوا . ٦ LM. من سراه, but M. in commentary سراها, which must be scanned ⏑ – ⏑.
٧ L. فى حرّ . ٨ L. وارفل and ارفالا . ١١ LM. الاشتياق .

XIX

١ يا طَلَلًا عِنْدَ ٱلأُثَيْلِ دارِسا * لاعَبْتُ فيه خُرَّدًا أَوانِسا

٢ بِٱلأَمْسِ كانَ مُؤْنِسًا وَضاحِكًا * وَٱليَوْمَ أَضْحَى مُوحِشًا وعابِسا

٣ نَأَوْا ولو أَشْعُرْ بِهِمْ فَما دَرَوْا * أَنَّ عَلَيْهِمْ مِنْ ضَمِيرِى حارِسا

٤ يَتْبَعُهُمْ حَيْثُ نَأَوْا وَخَيَّمُوا * وقد يَكُونُ لِلْمَطايا سايِسا

٥ حَتَّى إِذا حَلُّوا بِقَفْرٍ بَلْقَعٍ * وَخَيَّمُوا وَٱفْتَرَشُوا ٱلطَّنافِسا

٦ عادَ بِهِمْ رَوْضًا أَغَنَّ يانِعًا * مِنْ بَعْدِ ما قد كانَ قَفْرًا يابِسا

٧ ما نَزَلُوا فى مَنْزِلٍ إِلّا حَوَى * مِنَ ٱلحِسانِ رَوْضُهُ طَواوِسا

٨ وِلا نَأَوْا عن مَنْزِلٍ إِلّا حَوَتْ * مِن عاشِقِيهِمْ أَرْضُهُ نَواوِسا

٣ L. فلم اشعر ; L. من فوادى . ٧ LM. من منزل . ٨ LM. حوى .

XX

١ مَرَضِي مِنْ مَرِيضَةِ ٱلأَجْفَانِ * عَلِّلَانِي بِذِكْرِهَا عَلِّلَانِي

٢ هَفَتِ ٱلْوُرْقُ بِٱلرِّيَاضِ وَنَاحَتْ * شَجْوُ هٰذَا ٱلْحَمَامِ مِمَّا شَجَانِي

٣ بِأَبِي طَفْلَةٌ لَعُوبٌ تَهَادَى * مِنْ بَنَاتِ ٱلْخُدُورِ بَيْنَ ٱلْغَوَانِي

٤ طَلَعَتْ فى ٱلْعِيَانِ شَمْسًا فَلَمَّا * أَفَلَتْ أَشْرَقَتْ بِأُفْقِ جَنَانِي

٥ يَا طُلُولًا بِرَامَةٍ دَارِسَاتٍ * كَمْ رَأَتْ مِنْ كَوَاعِبٍ وَحِسَانِ

٦ بِأَبِي ثُمَّ بِي غَزَالٌ رَبِيبٌ * يَرْتَعِي بَيْنَ أَضْلُعِي فى أَمَانِ

٧ مَا عَلَيْهِ مِنْ نَارِهَا فَهْوَ نُورٌ * هٰكَذَا ٱلنُّورُ مُخْمِدُ ٱلنِّيرَانِ

٨ يَا خَلِيلَيَّ عَرِّجَا بِعِنَانِي * لِأَرَى رَسْمَ دَارِهَا بِعِيَانِي

٩ فَإِذَا مَا بَلَغْتُمَا ٱلدَّارَ حُطَّا * وَبِهَا صَاحِبَيَّ فَلْتَبْكِيَانِي

١٠ وَقِفَا بِي عَلَى ٱلطُّلُولِ قَلِيلًا * نَتَبَاكَى بَلْ أَبْكِ مِمَّا دَهَانِي

١١ ٱلْهَوَى رَاشِقِي بِغَيْرِ سِهَامٍ * ٱلْهَوَى قَاتِلِي بِغَيْرِ سِنَانِ

١٢ عَرِّفَانِي إِذَا بَكَيْتُ لَدَيْهَا * تُسْعِدَانِي عَلَى ٱلْبُكَا تُسْعِدَانِي

١٣ وَٱذْكُرَا لِي حَدِيثَ هِنْدٍ وَلُبْنَى * وَسُلَيْمَى وَزَيْنَبٍ وَعِنَانِ

١٤ ثُمَّ زِيدَا مِنْ حَاجِرٍ وَزَرُودٍ * خَبِّرَا عَنْ مَرَاتِعِ ٱلْغِزْلَانِ

١٥ وَٱنْدُبَانِي بِشِعْرِ قَيْسٍ وَلَيْلَى * وَبِمَيٍّ وَٱلْمُبْتَلَى غَيْلَانِ

١٦ طَالَ شَوْقِي لِطَفْلَةٍ ذَاتِ نَثْرٍ * وَنِظَامٍ وَمِنْبَرٍ وَبَيَانِ

١٧ مِنْ بَنَاتِ ٱلْمُلُوكِ مِنْ دَارِ فُرْسٍ * مِنْ أَجَلِّ ٱلْبِلَادِ مِنْ إِصْبَهَانِ

١٨ هِيَ بِنْتُ ٱلْعِرَاقِ بِنْتُ إِمَامِي * أَنَا ضِدُّهَا سَلِيلُ يَمَانِي

١٩ هَلْ رَأَيْتُمْ يَا سَادَتِي أَوْ سَمِعْتُمْ * أَنَّ ضِدَّيْنِ قَطُّ يَجْتَمِعَانِ

٢٠ لَوْ تَرَانَا بِرَامَةٍ نَتَعَاطَى * أَكْؤُسًا لِلْهَوَى بِغَيْرِ بَنَانِ

٢١ وَٱلْهَوَى بَيْنَنَا يَسُوقُ حَدِيثًا * طَيِّبًا مُطْرِبًا بِغَيْرِ لِسَانِ

٢٢ لَرَأَيْتُمْ مَا يَذْهَبُ ٱلْعَقْلُ فِيهِ * يَمَنٌ وَٱلْعِرَاقُ مُعْتَنِقَانِ

٤ M. فى الخيام. ٦ L. امانى. ٨ M. لا ارى. ٩ LMN. صاحباى.
١٠ L. عليها for قليلا. ١٢ LM. بكيت عليها. ١٨ LM. يمان.
٢١ N. يدير حديثا.

٢٣ كَذَبَ ٱلشَّاعِرُ ٱلَّذِى قَالَ قَبْلِى * وبِأَحْجَارِ عَقْلِهِ قد رَمَانِى

٢٤ أَيُّهَا ٱلْمُنْكِحُ ٱلثُّرَيَّا سُهَيْلًا * عَمْرَكَ ٱللَّهُ كَيْفَ يَلْتَقِيَانِ

٢٥ هِىَ شَامِيَّةٌ إِذَا مَا ٱسْتَقَلَّتْ * وسُهَيْلٌ إِذَا ٱسْتَقَلَّ يَمَانِى

XXI

١ أَيَا رَوْضَةَ الوادى أَجِبْ رَبَّةَ ٱلحِمَى * وذَاتَ الثَّنَايَا الغُرِّ يا رَوْضَةَ الوادى

٢ وظَلِّلْ عَلَيْهَا مِن ظِلَالِكَ سَاعَةً * قليلًا إِلى أَن يَسْتَقِرَّ بِهَا النادى

٣ وتُنْصَبَ بِٱلأَجْوَازِ منك خِيَامُهَا * فما شِئْتَ مِن طَلٍّ غِذَآءٍ لِمَبَادِ

٤ وما شِئْتَ مِن وَبْلٍ وما شِئْتَ مِن نَدًى * سَحَابٌ على بَانَاتِهَا رَايِحٌ غَادِى

٥ وما شِئْتَ مِن ظِلٍّ ظَلِيلٍ ومِن جَنًى * شَهِىٍّ لَدَى ٱلجَانِى يَمِيسُ بِمَيَّادِ

٦ ومِن نَاشِدٍ فيها زَرُودَ ورَمْلَهَا * ومِن مُنْشِدٍ حَادٍ ومِن مُرْشِدٍ هَادِى

٢ L. يستقلّ . ٣ N. بالاحواز ; LMN. ظال . ٦ MN. منشد for مرشد .

XXII

١ عُجْ بالرَّكَائِبِ نَحْوَ بُرْقَةِ ثَهْمَدِ * حَيْثُ ٱلقَضِيبُ الرَّطْبُ والرَّوْضُ النَّدِى

٢ حَيْثُ البُرُوقُ بِهَا تُرِيكَ وَمِيضَهَا * حَيْثُ السَّحَابُ بها يَرُوحُ ويَغْتَدِى

٣ وٱرْفَعْ صُوَيْتَكَ بالسُّحَيْرِ مُنَادِيًا * بالبِيضِ والغِيدِ الحِسَانِ الخُرَّدِ

٤ مِن كُلِّ فَاتِكَةٍ بِطَرْفٍ أَحْوَرٍ * مِن كُلِّ ثَانِيَةٍ بِجِيدٍ أَغْيَدِ

٥ تَهْوَى فتَقْصِدُ كُلَّ قَلْبٍ هَايِمٍ * يَهْوَى الحِسَانَ بِرَاشِقٍ ومُهَنَّدِ

٦ تَعْطُو بِرَخْصٍ كَٱلدِّمَقْسِ مُنَعَّمٍ * بِٱلنَّدِّ وٱلمِسْكِ ٱلفَتِيقِ مُقَرْمَدِ

٧ تَرْنُو إِذَا لَحَظَتْ بِمُقْلَةِ شَادِنٍ * يُعْزَى لِمُقْلَتِهَا سَوَادُ ٱلإِثْمِدِ

٨ بِٱلغُنْجِ وَٱلسِّحْرِ ٱلقَتُولِ مُكَحَّلٍ * بِٱلتِّيهِ وٱلحُسْنِ ٱلبَدِيعِ مُقَلَّدِ

٩ هَيْفَآءُ لا تَهْوَى ٱلَّذِى أَهْوَى ولا * تَفِى لِلَّذِى وَعَدَتْ بِصِدْقِ ٱلمَوْعِدِ

١٠ سَحَبَتْ غَدِيرَتَهَا شُجَاعًا أَسْوَدًا * لِتُخِيفَ مَنْ يَقْفُو بِذَاكَ ٱلأَسْوَدِ

١١ وٱللّٰهِ ما خِفْتُ ٱلمَنُونَ وإِنَّمَا * خَوْفِى أَمُوتُ فلا أَرَاهَا فى غَدِ

١ LM. تبمد . ٩ L. بالذى . ١٠ L. بدال الاسود ; M. has a lacuna here, extending from this verse to xxix, ٣.

XXIII

١ سُحَيْرًا أَنَاخُوا بِوادِى ٱلعَقِيقِ * وَقَدْ قَطَعُوا كُلَّ فَجٍّ عَمِيقِ

٢ فما طَلَعَ ٱلفَجْرُ إِلَّا وقَدْ * رَأَوْا عَلَمًا لَائِحًا فَوْقَ نِيقِ

٣ إذا رامَهُ ٱلنَّسْرُ لم يَسْتَطِعْ * فمِنْ دُونِهِ كانَ بَيْضُ ٱلأَنُوقِ

٤ عَلَيْهِ زَخارِفُ مَنْقُوشَةٌ * رَفِيعُ ٱلقَواعِدِ مِثْلُ ٱلعَقُوقِ

٥ وقَدْ كَتَبُوا أَسْطُرًا أَوْدِعُوها * أَلَا مَنْ لِصَبٍّ غَرِيبٍ مَشُوقِ

٦ لَهُ هِمَّةٌ فَوْقَ هٰذا ٱلسِماكِ * ويُوطَأُ بِٱلْخُفِّ وَطْأَ ٱلحَرِيقِ

٧ ومَسْكَنُهُ عِنْدَ ذا ٱلعُقابِ * وقَدْ ماتَ بِٱلدَّمْعِ مَوْتَ ٱلغَرِيقِ

٨ قَدَ ٱسْلَمَهُ ٱلحُبُّ لِلحادِثاتِ * بِهٰذا ٱلمَكانِ بِغَيْرِ شَفِيقِ

٩ فيا وارِدِينَ مِياهَ ٱلقَلِيبِ * ويا ساكِنِينَ بِوادِى ٱلعَقِيقِ

١٠ ويا طالِبًا طَيْبَةً زايِرًا * ويا سالِكِينَ بِهٰذا ٱلطَّرِيقِ

١١ أَفِيقُوا عَلَيْنا فإِنَّا رُزِينا * بُعَيْدَ ٱلسُّحَيْرِ قُبَيْلَ ٱلشُّرُوقِ

١٢ بِبَيْضاءَ غَيْداءَ بَهْنانَةٍ * تَضَوَّعُ نَشْرًا كَمِسْكٍ فَتِيقِ

١٣ تَمايَلُ سَكْرَى كَمِثْلِ ٱلغُصُونِ * ثَنَتْها الرِّياحُ كَمِثْلِ ٱلشَّقِيقِ

١٤ بِرِدْفٍ مَهُولٍ كَدِعْصِ ٱلنَّقا * تَرَجْرَجُ مِثْلَ سَنامِ ٱلفَنِيقِ

١٥ فما لامَنِى فى هَواها عَذُولٌ * ولا لامَنِى فى هَواها صَدِيقِ

١٦ ولَوْ لامَنِى فى هَواها عَذُولٌ * لَكانَ جَوابِى إِلَيْهِ شَهِيقِ

١٧ فشَوْقِى رِكابِى وحُزْنِى لِباسِى * ووَجْدِى صَبُوحِى ودَمْعِى غَبُوقِ

٥ L. اودعوا ابها; L. غريب شفوق. ٦ L. وطى. ٧ L. فى الدمع.
١٤ L. العنيق. ١٦ L. الشهيق.

XXIV

قال وانشدنى بعض الفقراء بيتًا لا اعرف له اخًا وهو هذا

كُلُّ ٱلَّذِى يَرْجُو نَوالَكِ أُمْطِرُوا * ما كان بَرْقُكِ خُلَّبًا إِلَّا مَعِى

فاعجبنى معزاه وتفوت معناه فعملت ابياتًا فى هذا الروى وضمنتها هذا البيت بكماله اجابةً لذالك الفقير رحمه الله تعالى فقلت

١ قِفْ بِٱلطُّلولِ ٱلدّارِساتِ بِلَعْلَعِ * وَٱنْدُبْ أُحِبَّتَنا بِذاكَ ٱلبَلْقَعِ

٢ قِفْ بِٱلدِّيارِ ونادِها مُتَعَجِّبًا * مِنْها بِحُسْنِ تَلَطُّفٍ بِتَفَجُّعِ

٣ عَهْدى بِمِثْلى عِنْدَ بانِكِ قاطِفًا * ثَمَرَ ٱلقُدُودِ وَوَرْدَ رَوْضٍ أَيْنَعِ

٤ كُلُّ ٱلَّذى يَرْجو نَوالَكِ أُمْطِرُوا * ما كانَ بَرْقُكِ خُلَّبًا إلّا مَعى

٥ قالَتْ نَعَمْ قَدْ كانَ ذاكَ ٱلمُلْتَقى * فى ظِلِّ أَفْنانى بِأَخْصَبِ مَوْضِعِ

٦ إذْ كانَ بَرْقى من بُرُوقِ مَباسِمٍ * وَٱليَوْمَ بَرْقى لَمْعُ هٰذا اليَرْمَعِ

٧ فٱعْتِبْ زَمانًا ما لَنا من حيلَةٍ * فى دَفْعِهِ ما ذَنْبُ مَنْزِلِ لَعْلَعِ

٨ فَعَذَرْتُها لَمّا سَمِعْتُ كَلامَها * تَشْكو كَما أَشْكو بِقَلْبٍ مُوجَعِ

٩ وَسَأَلْتُها لَمّا رَأَيْتُ رُبُوعَها * مَسْرى ٱلرِّياحِ ٱلذّارِياتِ ٱلأَرْبَعِ

١٠ هَلْ أَخْبَرَتْكِ رِياحُهُمْ بِمَقيلِهِمْ * قالَتْ نَعَمْ قالُوا بِذاتِ ٱلأَجْرَعِ

١١ حَيْثُ ٱلخِيامُ ٱلبِيضُ تُشْرِقُ بِٱلَّذى * تَحْوِيهِ مِنْ تِلْكَ ٱلشُّمُوسِ ٱلطُّلَّعِ

٨ L. جوابها.

XXV

١ وا حَرَبا مِنْ كَبِدى وا حَرَبا * وا طَرَبا مِنْ خَلَدى وا طَرَبا

٢ فى كَبِدى نارُ جَوًى مُحْرِقَةٌ * فى خَلَدى بَدْرُ دُجًى قد غَرَبا

٣ يا مِسْكُ يا بَدْرُ ويا غُصْنَ نَقًا * ما أَوْرَقا ما أَنْوَرا ما أَطْيَبا

٤ يا مَبْسِمًا أَحْبَبْتُ منه ٱلحَبَبا * ويا رُضابًا ذُقْتُ منه ٱلضَّرَبا

٥ يا قَمَرًا فى شَفَقٍ من خَفَرٍ * فى خَدِّهِ لاحَ لَنا مُنْتَقِبا

٦ لَوْ أَنَّهُ يُسْفِرُ عن بُرْقُعِهِ * كانَ عَذابًا فَلِهٰذا ٱحْتَجَبا

٧ شَمْسُ ضُحًى فى فَلَكٍ طالِعَةٌ * غُصْنُ نَقًى فى رَوْضَةٍ قد نُصِبا

٨ ظِلْتُ لَبًا من حَذَرٍ مُرْتَقِبًا * وَٱلغُصْنُ أَسْقِيهِ سَماءً صَيِّبا

٩ إنْ طَلَعَتْ كانَتْ لِعَيْنى عَجَبًا * او غَرَبَتْ كانَتْ لِحَيْنى سَبَبا

١٠ مُذْ عَقَدَ ٱلحُسْنُ على مَفْرِقِها * تاجًا من التِّبْرِ عَشِقْتُ ٱلذَّهَبا

٣ L. ما اورق ما انوره. ٨ L. والحسن اسعته.

١١ لَوْ أَنَّ إِبْلِيسَ رَأَى مِنْ آدَمٍ * نُورَ مُحَيَّاهَا عَلَيْهِ مَا أَبَى
١٢ لَوْ أَنَّ إِدْرِيسَ رَأَى مَا رَقَمَ * ٱلْحُسْنُ بِخَدَّيْهَا إِذًا مَا كَتَبَا
١٣ لَوْ أَنَّ بِلْقِيسَ رَأَتْ، رَفْرَفَهَا * مَا خَطَرَ ٱلْعَرْشُ وَلَا ٱلصَّرْحُ بِبَا
١٤ يَا سَرْحَةَ ٱلْوَادِى وَيَا بَانَ ٱلْغَضَا * أَهْدُوا لَنَا مِنْ نَشْرِكُمْ مَعَ ٱلصَّبَا
١٥ مُمَسَّكًا يَفُوحُ رَيَّاهُ لَنَا * مِنْ زَهْرِ أَهْضَامِكَ أَوْ زَهْرِ ٱلرُّبَى
١٦ يَا بَانَةَ ٱلْوَادِى أَرِينَا فَنَنًا * فِى لِينِ أَعْطَافٍ لَهَا أَوْ قُضُبَا
١٧ رِيحُ صَبًا تُخْبِرُ عَنْ عَصْرِ صِبًا * بِحَاجِرٍ أَوْ بِمِنًى أَوْ بِقُبَا
١٨ أَوْ بِٱلنَّقَا فَٱلْمُنْحَنَى عِنْدَ ٱلْحِمَى * أَوْ لَعْلَعٍ حَيْثُ مَرَاتِعُ ٱلظِّبَا
١٩ لَا تَعْجَبَنْ لَا عَجَبًا * مِنْ عَرَبِيٍّ يَتَهَاوَى ٱلْعُرُبَا
٢٠ يَفْنَى إِذَا مَا صَدَحَتْ قُمْرِيَّةٌ * بِذِكْرِ مَنْ يَهْوَاهُ فِيهِ طَرَبَا

١٣ L. زفرتها . ١٤ L. اهدى ; L. نشرها . ١٥ L. اهضابک .
١٨ L. والمنحنى . ٢٠ L. حدثت ; L. هواه .

XXVI

١ بِٱلْجِزْعِ بَيْنَ ٱلْأَبْرَقَيْنِ ٱلْمَوْعِدُ * فَأَنِخْ رِكَابَنَا فَهٰذَا ٱلْمَوْرِدُ
٢ لَا تَطْلُبَنَّ وَلَا تُنَادِى بَعْدَهُ * يَا بَارِقٌ يَا حَاجِرٌ يَا ثَهْمَدُ
٣ وَٱلْعَبْ كَمَا لَعِبَتْ أَوَانِسُ نُهَّدٌ * وَٱرْتَعْ كَمَا رَتَعَتْ ظِبَاءٌ شُرَّدُ
٤ فِى رَوْضَةٍ غَنَّى وَصَاحَ ذُبَابُهَا * فَأَجَابَهُ طَرَبًا هُنَاكَ مُغَرِّدُ
٥ رَقَّتْ حَوَاشِيهَا وَرَقَّ نَسِيمُهَا * فَٱلْغَيْمُ يَبْرُقُ وَٱلْغَمَامَةُ تَرْعَدُ
٦ وَالْوَدْقُ يَنْزِلُ مِنْ خِلَالِ سَحَابِهِ * كَدُمُوعِ صَبٍّ لِلْفِرَاقِ تَبَدَّدُ
٧ وَٱشْرَبْ سُلَافَةَ خَمْرِهَا بِخُمَارِهَا * وَٱطْرَبْ عَلَى غَرِدٍ هُنَالِكَ يُنْشِدُ
٨ وَسُلَافَةٍ فِى عَهْدِ آدَمَ أَخْبَرَتْ * عَنْ جَنَّةِ ٱلْمَأْوَى حَدِيثًا يُسْنَدُ
٩ إِنَّ ٱلْحِسَانَ نَقَلْنَهَا مِنْ رِيقِهَا * كَٱلْمِسْكِ جَادَ بِهَا عَلَيْنَا ٱلْخُرَّدُ

٨ L. من عهد . ٩ L. om. this verse.

XXVII

١ يا أَيُّـهـا ٱلبَيْتُ ٱلعَتِيقُ تَـعـالَى * نُـورٌ لَـكُـمْ بِقُلُوبِنا يَـتَـلالا

٢ أَشْكُو إِلَيْكَ مَفاوِزًا قد جُبْتُها * أَرْسَلْتُ فيها أَدْمُعِى إِرْسالا

٣ أُمْسِى وأُصْبِحُ لا أَلَذُّ بِراحةٍ * أَصِلُ ٱلبُكُورَ وأَقْطَعُ ٱلآصالا

٤ إِنّ ٱلنِّياقَ وإِنْ أَضَرَّ بِها ٱلوَجَى * تَسْرِى وتُرْقِلُ فى ٱلسُّرَى إِرْقالا

٥ هٰذِى ٱلرِّكابُ إِلَيْكُمْ سارَتْ بِنا * شَوْقًا وما تَرْجُو بذاك وِصالا

٦ قَطَعَتْ إِلَيْكَ سَباسِبًا ورِئالا * وَجْدًا وما تَشْكُو لِذاكَ كَلالا

٧ ما تَشْتَكِى أَلَمَ ٱلجَوَى وأَنا ٱلّذِى * أَشْكُو ٱلكَلالَ لَقَدْ أَتَيْتُ مُحالا

٥ L. وما تبغى . ٦ N. ورمالا ; L. ولا تشكو.

XXVIII

١ بَيْنَ ٱلنَّقا ولَعْلَعِ * ظِباءُ ذاتِ ٱلأَجْرَعِ

٢ تَرْعَى بِها فى خَمَرٍ * خَمايِلًا وتَرْتَعِى

٣ ما طَلَعَتْ أَهِلَّةٌ * بِأُفْقِ ذاكَ ٱلمَطْلَعِ

٤ إِلّا وَدَدْتُ أَنَّها * مِن حَذَرٍ لَمْ تَطْلُعِ

٥ ولا بَدَتْ لامِعَةٌ * مِنْ بَرْقِ ذاكَ ٱليَرْمَعِ

٦ إِلّا ٱشْتَهَيْتُ أَنَّها * لِما بِنا لم تَلْمَعِ

٧ يا دَمْعَتِى وٱنْسَكِبِى * يا مُقْلَتِى لا تُقْلِعِى

٨ يا زَفْرَتِى خُذْ صُعُدًا * يا كَبِدِى تَصَدَّعِى

٩ وأَنْتَ يا حادِى ٱتَّئِدْ * فٱلنّارُ بَيْنَ أَضْلُعِى

١٠ قد فَنِيَتْ مِمّا جَرَى * خَوْفَ ٱلفِراقِ أَدْمُعِى

١١ حَتّى إِذا حَلَّ ٱلنَّوَى * لم تَلْقَ عَيْنًا تَدْمَعُ

١٢ فٱرْحَلْ إِلَى وادِى ٱللِّوَى * مَرْبَعِهِمْ ومَصْرَعِى

١٣ إِنَّ بِهِ أَحِبَّتِى * عِنْدَ مِياهِ ٱلأَجْرَعِ

٥ N. in marg. خلف for برق . ٦ L. الّا وددت . ١١ L. تدمعى .

١٤ ونادِهِمْ مَنْ لِفَتًى * ذى لَوْعَةٍ مُوَدِّعِ

١٥ رَمَتْ بِهِ أَشْجانُهُ * بَهْمآءَ رَسْمَ بَلْقَعِ

١٦ يا قَمَرًا تَحْتَ ٱلدُّجَى * خُذْ منه شَيْئًا ودَعِ

١٧ وزَوِّدِيهِ نَظْرَةً * من خَلْفِ ذاكَ ٱلْبُرْقُعِ

١٨ لِأَنَّهُ يَضْعُفُ عن * دَرْكِ ٱلْجَمالِ ٱلْأَرْوَعِ

١٩ او عَلِّلِيهِ بِٱلْمُنَى * عساهُ يُحْيَى او يَعِى

٢٠ ما هُوَ إِلّا مَيِّتٌ * بَيْنَ ٱلنَّقا ولَعْلَعِ

٢١ فَمِتُّ يأسًا وأَسًى * كما أَنا فى مَوْضِعِى

٢٢ ما صَدَقَتْ رِيحُ ٱلصَّبا * حِينَ أَتَتْ بِٱلْخُدَعِ

٢٣ قد تَكْذِبُ ٱلرِّيحُ إذا * تُسْمِعُ ما لم يُسْمَعِ

XXIX

١ بِأَبِى ٱلْغُصُونُ المايِساتُ عَواطِفَا * اَلْعاطِفاتُ على ٱلْخُدُودِ سَوالِفا

٢ اَلْمُرْسِلاتُ مِنَ ٱلشُّعورِ غَدايِرًا * اَللَّيِّناتُ مَعاقِدًا ومَعاطِفا

٣ اَلسّاحِباتُ مِنَ الدَّلالِ ذَلاذِلًا * اَللّابِساتُ مِنَ ٱلْجَمالِ مَطارِفا

٤ اَلْباخِلاتُ بِحُسْنِهِنَّ صِيانَةً * اَلْواهِباتُ مَتالِدًا ومَطارِفا

٥ اَلْمُؤْنِقاتُ مَضاحِكًا ومَباسِمًا * اَلطَّيِّباتُ مُقَبَّلًا ومَراشِفا

٦ اَلنّاعِماتُ مُجَرَّدًا وَٱلْكاعِبا * تُ مُنَهَّدًا والمُهْدِياتُ طَرايِفا

٧ اَلْجالِباتُ بِكُلِّ سِحْرٍ مُعْجِبٍ * عِنْدَ ٱلْحَدِيثِ مَسامِعًا ولَطايِفا

٨ اَلسّاتِراتُ مِنَ ٱلْحَيآءِ مَحاسِنًا * تَسْبِى بِها ٱلْقَلْبَ ٱلتَّقِىَّ ٱلْخايِفا

٩ اَلْمُبْدِياتُ مِنَ ٱلثُّغُورِ لَآلِيًا * تَشْفِى بِرِيقَتِها ضَعِيفًا تالِفا

١٠ اَلرّامِياتُ مِنَ ٱلْعُيُونِ رَواشِقًا * قَلْبًا خَبِيرًا بِٱلْحُرُوبِ مُثاقِفا

١١ اَلْمُطْلِعاتُ مِنَ ٱلْجُيُوبِ أَهِلَّةً * لا تُلْفَيَنَّ مَعَ ٱلتَّمامِ كَواسِفا

١٢ اَلْمُنْشِئاتُ مِنَ ٱلدُّمُوعِ سَحايِبًا * اَلْمُسْمِعاتُ مِنَ ٱلزَّفِيرِ قَواصِفا

٥ M. تضاحكا.   ٦ N. ظرايفا.   ٧ L. وملاطفا.   ٨ M. النقى.
١١ LMN. يلفين.

١٣ يا صاحِبَيَّ بمُهْجتي خُمْصانةٌ * أَسْدَتْ إِلَيَّ أيادِيًا وعَوارِفا

١٤ نَظَمَتْ نِظامَ الشَّمْلِ فَهْيَ نِظامُنا * عَرَبِيَّةٌ عَجْماءُ تُلْهِى ٱلعارِفا

١٥ مَهْما رَنَتْ سَلَّتْ عَلَيْكَ صَوارِمًا * ويُرِيكَ مَبْسِمُها بَرِيقًا خاطِفا

١٦ يا صاحِبَىَّ قِفا بِأَكْنافِ ٱلحِمَى * مِنْ حاجِرٍ يا صاحِبَىَّ قِفا قِفا

١٧ حتّى أُسائِلَ أَيْنَ مالَتْ عِيسُهُمْ * فَقَدِ ٱقْتَحَمْتُ مَعاطِبًا ومَتالِفا

١٨ ومَعالِمًا ومَجاهِلًا بِشِمِلَّةٍ * تَشْكُو الوَجَى وسَباسِبًا وتَنايِفا

١٩ مَطْوِيَّةِ الأَقْرابِ أَذْهَبَ سَيْرُها * بِحَشِيشِهِ منها قُوًى وسَدايِفا

٢٠ حتّى وَقَفْتُ بِها بِرَمْلَةِ حاجِرٍ * فرَأَيْتُ نُوقًا بِٱلأُثَيْلِ خَوالِفا

٢١ يَقْتادُها قَمَرٌ عَلَيْهِ مَهابَةٌ * فطَوَيْتُ مِن حَذَرٍ عَلَيْهِ شَراسِفا

٢٢ قَمَرٌ تَعَرَّضَ فى ٱلطَّوافِ فلم أَكُنْ * بِسِواهُ عِنْدَ طَوافِهِ بى طايِفا

٢٣ يَمْحُو بِفاضِلِ بُرْدِهِ آثارَهُ * فتَحارُ لَوْ كُنْتَ ٱلدَّلِيلَ ٱلقايِفا

١٨ M. الوحى . ٢٠ L. برملة عالج . ٢١ L. حذرى .
٢٢ L. به طايفا ; M. من طايفا .

XXX

١ بِأُثَيْلاتِ ٱلنَّقا سِرْبُ قَطًا * ضَرَبَ ٱلحُسْنُ عَلَيْهِ طُنُبا

٢ وبِأَجْوازِ ٱلفَلا مِن إِضَمٍ * نَعَمٌ تَرْعَى لَدَيْها وظِبا

٣ يا خَلِيلَيَّ قِفا وٱسْتَنْطِقا * رَسْمَ دارٍ بَعْدَهُمْ قد خَرِبا

٤ وٱنْدُبا قَلْبَ فَتًى فارَقَهُ * يَوْمَ بانُوا وٱبْكِيا وٱنْتَحِبا

٥ عَلَّهُ يُخْبِرُ حَيْثُ يَمَّمُوا * أَلِجَرْعاءِ ٱلحِمَى أَمْ لِقُبا

٦ رَحَلوا ٱلعِيسَ ولم أَشْعُرْ بِهِمْ * أَلِسَهْوٍ كانَ أَمْ طَرْفٍ نَبا

٧ لم يَكُنْ ذاكَ ولا هٰذا وما * كانَ إلّا وَلَهٌ قد غَلَبا

٨ يا هُمُومًا شَرَدَتْ وٱفْتَرَقَتْ * خَلْفَهُمْ تَطْلُبُهُمْ أَيْدى سَبا

٩ أَىَّ رِيحٍ نَسَمَتْ نادَيْتُها * يا شَمالًا يا جَنُوبًا يا صَبا

٢ N. وباجوار ; L. وباجواز . ٥ M. الجرعا والحما .

١٠ هَلْ لَدَيْكُمْ خَبَرٌ مِمَّا بِنَا * قد لَقِينَا مِنْ نَوَاهُمْ نَصَبَا
١١ أَسْنَدَتْ رِيحُ ٱلصَّبَا أَخْبَارَهَا * عن نَبَاتِ ٱلشِّيحِ عن زَهْرِ الرُّبَى
١٢ أَنَّ مَنْ أَمْرَضَهُ دَآءُ ٱلْهَوَى * فَلْيُعَلَّلْ بِأَحَادِيثِ ٱلصِّبَا
١٣ ثُمَّ قَالَتْ يا شَمَالُ خَبِّرِى * مِثْلَ ما خَبَّرْتُهُ او أَعْجَبَا
١٤ ثُمَّ أَنْتِ يا جَنُوبُ حَدِّثِى * مِثْلَ ما حَدَّثْتُهُ او أَعْذَبَا
١٥ قالَت ٱلشَّمْأَلُ عِنْدِى فَرَجٌ * شارَكَتْ فيه ٱلشَّمالُ ٱلْأَزْيَبَا
١٦ كُلُّ سُوءٍ فى هَوَاهُمْ حَسَنٌ * وعَذابى بِرِضاهُمْ عَذُبَا
١٧ فإِلَى مَ وعلى مَ ولِمَا * تَشْتَكِى ٱلْبَثَّ وتَشْكُو ٱلْوَصَبَا
١٨ وإذا ما وَعَدُوكُمْ ما تَرَى * بَرْقَهُ إلّا بُرَيْقًا خُلَّبَا
١٩ رَقَمَ ٱلْغَيْمُ على رُدْنِ ٱلْغَمَى * مِنْ سَنَا ٱلْبَرْقِ طِرَازًا مُذْهَبَا
٢٠ فَجَرَتْ أَدْمُعُهَا مِنْهَا عَلَى * صَحْنِ خَدَّيْهَا فَأَذْكَتْ لَهَبَا
٢١ وَرْدَةٌ نَابِتَةٌ مِنْ أَدْمُعٍ * نَرْجِسٌ يَمْطُرُ غَيْثًا عَجَبَا
٢٢ وَمَتَى رُمْتَ جَنَاهَا أَرْسَلَتْ * عِطْفُ صُدْغَيْهَا عَلَيْهَا عَقْرَبَا
٢٣ تَشْرُقُ ٱلشَّمْسُ إذا ما ٱبْتَسَمَتْ * رَبِّ ما أَنْوَرَ ذاكَ الحَبَبَا
٢٤ يَطْلُعُ ٱللَّيْلُ إذا ما أَسْدَلَتْ * فاحِمًا جَثْلًا أَثِيثًا غَيْهَبَا
٢٥ يَتَجَارَى ٱلنَّحْلُ مَهْمَا تَفَلَتْ * رَبِّ ما أَعْذَبَ ذاكَ الشَّنَبَا
٢٦ وإذا مالَتْ أَرَتْنَا فَنَنًا * او رَنَتْ سَلَّتْ مِنَ ٱللَّحْظِ ظُبَى
٢٧ كَمْ تُنَاغِى بِٱلنَّقَا مِنْ حاجِرٍ * يا سَلِيلَ ٱلعَرَبِىّ ٱلعُرُبَا
٢٨ أَنَا إلّا عَرَبِىٌّ ولِذا * أَعْشَقُ ٱلْبِيضَ وأَهْوَى ٱلْعُرُبَا
٢٩ لا أُبَالِى شَرَقَ ٱلْوَجْدُ بِنَا * حَيْثُ ما كانَتْ بِهِ او غَرَبَا
٣٠ كُلَّمَا قُلْتُ أَلا قالُوا أَمَا * وإذا ما قُلْتُ هَلْ قالُوا أَبَى

١٠ L. om. this verse. ١٤ LN. انتى . ١٥ N. فرح .
١٦ LM. وعذاب . ١٧ M. فالى ما . ١٩ N. الغمام ; L. الغما ;
N. هذا الحببا , but ذاك in marg. ٢٤ N. تُطلع .
٢٥ M. يتهادى ; M. ممّا تفلت . ٢٨ Sir Charles Lyall suggests
آنا (= أَأَنا) for أَنا , but cf. XV, ٨ .

٣١ وَمَتَى ما أَنْجَدُوا او أَتْهَمُوا * أَقْطَعُ ٱلْبِيدا أَحُثُّ ٱلطَّلَبا

٣٢ سامِرِيُّ ٱلْوَقْتِ قَلْبِي كُلَّما * أَبْصَرَ ٱلآثارَ يَبْغِي ٱلْمَذْهَبا

٣٣ فَإِذا هُمْ شَرَّقُوا او غَرَّبُوا * كانَ ذا ٱلْقَرْنَيْنِ يَقْفُو ٱلسَّبَبا

٣٤ كَمْ دَعَوْنا لِوِصالٍ رَغَبًا * كَمْ دَعَوْنا مِن فِراقٍ رَهَبا

٣٥ يا بَنِي ٱلزَّوْراءِ هٰذا قَمَرٌ * عِنْدَكُمْ لاحَ وَعِنْدِي غَرَبا

٣٦ حَرَبِي وَٱللهِ مِنْهُ حَرَبِي * كَمْ أُنادِي خَلْفَهُ وا حَرَبا

٣٧ لَهْفَ نَفْسِي لَهْفَ نَفْسِي لِفَتًى * كُلَّما غَنَّى حَمامٌ غُيِّبا

XXXI

١ أَضاءَ بِذاتِ ٱلأَضا بارِقُ * وَمِنَ ٱلنُّورِ فى جَوِّها خافِقُ

٢ وَصَلْصَلَ رَعْدُ مُناجاتِهِ * فَأَرْسَلَ مِدْرارَهُ ٱلْوادِقُ

٣ تَنادَوْا أَنِيخُوا فَلَمْ يَسْمَعُوا * فَصِحْتُ مِنَ ٱلْوَجْدِ يا سايِقُ

٤ أَلا فَٱنْزِلُوا هاهُنا وَٱرْبَعُوا * فَإِنِّى بِمَنْ عِنْدَكُمْ وامِقُ

٥ بِهَيْفاءَ غَيْداءَ رُعْبُوبَةٍ * فُؤادُ ٱلشَّجِيِّ لَها تايِقُ

٦ يَفُوحُ ٱلنَّدِيُّ لَدَى ذِكْرِها * فَكُلُّ لِسانٍ بِها ناطِقُ

٧ فَلَوْ أَنَّ مَجْلِسَها هَضْبَةٌ * وَمَقْعَدُها جَبَلٌ حالِقُ

٨ لَكانَ ٱلْقَرارُ بِها حالِقًا * وَلَنْ يُدْرِكَ ٱلحالِقَ ٱلرّامِقُ

٩ فَكُلُّ خَرابٍ بِها عامِرٌ * وَكُلُّ سَرابٍ بِها غادِقُ

١٠ وَكُلُّ رِياضٍ بِها زاهِرٌ * وَكُلُّ شَرابٍ بِها رايِقُ

١١ فَلَيْلِى مِنْ وَجْهِها مُشْرِقٌ * وَيَوْمِى مِنْ شَعْرِها غاسِقُ

١٢ لَقَدْ فَتَقَتْ حَبَّةَ ٱلْقَلْبِ إِذْ * رَماها بِأَسْهُمِها ٱلْفالِقُ

١٣ عُيُونٌ تَعَوَّدْنَ رَشْقَ ٱلحَشا * فَلَيْسَ يَطِيشُ لَها راشِقُ

١٤ فَما هامَةٌ فى خَرابِ ٱلبِقاعِ * وَلا ساقُ حُرٍّ وَلا ناعِقُ

٤ M. وارتعوا . ٦ M. لذى ذكرها . ٧ L. هضبة . ١٣ M. رتق الحشى .
١٤ M. خراب القياع .

١٥ بِأَشْأَمَ مِنْ بَازِلٍ رَحَّلُوا * لِيَحْمِلَ مَنْ حُسْنُهُ فَائِقُ
١٦ وَيَتْرُكَ صَبًّا بِذَاتِ ٱلْأَضَا * قَتِيلًا وَفِى حُبِّهِمْ صَادِقُ

XXXII

١ يُذَكِّرُنِى حَالَ ٱلشَّبِيبَةِ وَٱلشَّرْخِ * حَدِيثٌ لَنَا بَيْنَ ٱلْحَدِيثَةِ وَٱلْكَرْخِ
٢ فَقُلْتُ لِنَفْسِى بَعْدَ خَمْسِينَ حِجَّةً * وَقَدْ صِرْتُ مِنْ طُولِ ٱلتَّفَكُّرِ كَٱلْفَرْخِ
٣ يُذَكِّرُنِى أَكْنَافَ سَلْعٍ وَحَاجِرٍ * وَيَذْكُرُ لِى حَالَ ٱلشَّبِيبَةِ وَٱلشَّرْخِ
٤ وَسَوْقِى ٱلْمَطَايَا مُنْجِدًا ثُمَّ مُتْهِمًا * وَقَدْحِى لَهَا نَارَ ٱلْعَفَارِ مَعَ ٱلْمَرْخِ

٣ M. تذكرنى ; L. اعلام سلع ; M. وتذكرنى. ٤ N. وسوق.

XXXIII

١ أُطَارِحُ كُلَّ هَاتِفَةٍ بِأَيْكٍ * عَلَى فَنَنٍ بِأَفْنَانِ ٱلشُّجُونِ
٢ فَتَبْكِى إِلْفَهَا مِنْ غَيْرِ دَمْعٍ * وَدَمْعُ ٱلْحُزْنِ تَهْمُلُ مِنْ جُفُونِى
٣ أَقُولُ لَهَا وَقَدْ سَمَحَتْ جُفُونِى * بِأَدْمُعِهَا تُخَبِّرُ عَنْ شُؤُونِى
٤ أَعِنْدَكِ بِٱلَّذِى أَهْوَاهُ عِلْمٌ * وَهَلْ قَالُوا بِأَفْيَاءِ ٱلْغُصُونِ

٣ M. سمحت.

XXXIV

١ عِنْدَ ٱلْكَثِيبِ مِنْ جِبَالِ زَرُودِ * صِيدٌ وَأُسْدٌ مِنْ لِحَاظِ ٱلْغِيدِ
٢ صَرْعَى وَهُمْ أَبْنَاءُ مَلْحَمَةِ ٱلْوَغَى * أَيْنَ ٱلْأُسُودُ مِنَ ٱلْعُيُونِ ٱلسُّودِ
٣ فَتَكَتْ بِهِمْ لَحَظَاتُهُنَّ وَحَبَّذَا * تِلْكَ ٱلْمَلَاحِظُ مِنْ بَنَاتِ ٱلصِّيدِ

XXXV

١ ثَلَاثُ بُدُورٍ مَا يُزَنَّ بِزِينَةٍ * خَرَجْنَ إِلَى ٱلتَّنْعِيمِ مُعْتَجِرَاتِ
٢ حَسَرْنَ عَنَ آمْثَالِ ٱلشُّمُوسِ إِضَاءَةً * وَلَبَّيْنَ بِٱلْإِهْلَالِ مُعْتَمِرَاتِ
٣ وَأَقْبَلْنَ يَمْشِينَ ٱلرُّوَيْدَا كَمِثْلِ مَا * تَمَشَّى ٱلْقَطَا فِى أَلْحُفِ ٱلْحِبَرَاتِ

١ L. ما برزن لريبة ; M. ما برزن بريبة. ٣ L. الرويد.

XXXVI

١ أَلا يا ثَرَى نَجْدٍ تَبارَكْتَ مِن نَجْدِ * سَقَتْكَ سَحابُ ٱلْمُزْنِ جَوْدًا عَلَى جَوْدِ

٢ وحَيّاكَ مَنْ حَيّاكَ خَمْسينَ حِجَّةً * بِعَوْدٍ عَلَى بَدْءٍ وبَدْءٍ عَلَى عَوْدِ

٣ قَطَعْتُ إِلَيْها كُلَّ قَفْرٍ ومَهْمَهٍ * عَلَى ٱلنّاقَةِ ٱلْكَوْماءِ وٱلْجَمَلِ ٱلْعَوْدِ

٤ إِلَى أَنْ تَراءَى ٱلْبَرْقُ مِنْ جانِبِ ٱلْغَضا * وقَدْ زادَنى مَسْراهُ وَجْدًا عَلَى وَجْدى

¹ N. in marg. سقاك . ² LM. من احياك .

XXXVII

١ يا خَليلَيَّ أَلِمّا بِٱلْحِمَى * وٱطْلُبا نَجْدًا وذاكَ ٱلْعَلَما

٢ ورِدا ماءً بِخَيْماتِ ٱللِّوَى * وٱسْتَظِلّا ضالَها وٱلسَّلَما

٣ فإِذا ما جِئْتُما وادِى مِنًى * فٱلَّذى قَلْبى بِهِ قَدْ جِئْتُما

٤ أَبْلِغا عَنّى تَحِيّاتِ ٱلْهَوَى * كُلَّ مَنْ حَلَّ بِهِ او سَلِما

٥ وٱسْمَعا ما ذا يُجيبُونَ بِهِ * وٱخْبِرا عَنْ دَنِفِ ٱلْقَلْبِ بِما

٦ يَشْتَكيهِ مِنْ صَباباتِ ٱلْهَوَى * مُعْلِمًا مُسْتَخْبِرًا مُسْتَفْهِما

XXXVIII

١ أُحِبُّ بِلادِ ٱللّٰهِ لى بَعْدَ طَيْبَةٍ * ومَكَّةَ وٱلْأَقْصَى مَدِينَةَ بَغْدانِ

٢ وما لِيَ لا أَهْوَى ٱلسَّلامَ ولى بِها * إِمامُ هُدًى دِينى وعَقْلى وإِيمانى

٣ فقَدْ سَكَنَتْها مِنْ بُنَيّاتِ فارِسٍ * لَطِيفَةُ إِيماءٍ مَرِيضَةُ أَجْفانِ

٤ تُحَيّى فتُحْيى مَنْ أَماتَتْ بِلَحْظِها * فجاءَتْ بِحُسْنَى بَعْدَ حُسْنٍ وإِحْسانِ

¹ M. بغداد . ² LMN. وعقدى . ³ LM. وقد ; M. بنات لفارس .

XXXIX

١ نَفْسى ٱلْفِداءُ لِبِيضٍ خُرَّدٍ عُرُبٍ * لَعِبْنَ بى عِنْدَ لَثْمِ ٱلرُّكْنِ وٱلْحَجَرِ

٢ ما تَسْتَدِلُّ إِذا ما تِهْتَ خَلْفَهُمُ * إِلّا بِرِيحِهِمُ مِنْ أَطْيَبِ ٱلْأَثَرِ

٣ ولا دَجَى بِىَ لَيْلٌ ما بِهِ قَمَرٌ * إلّا ذَكَرْتُهُمُ فَسِرْتُ فى ٱلْقَمَرِ
٤ وإنّما حِينَ أَمْشى فى رِكابِهِمُ * فَٱللَّيْلُ عِنْدِى مِثْلُ الشَّمْسِ فى ٱلْبُكَرِ
٥ غازَلْتُ مِنْ غَزَلى مِنْهُنَّ واحِدَةً * حَسْناءَ لَيْسَ لَها أُخْتٌ مِنَ ٱلْبَشَرِ
٦ إنْ أَسْفَرَتْ عَنْ مُحَيّاها أَرَتْكَ سَنًا * مِثْلَ ٱلْغَزالَةِ إشْراقًا بِلا غِيَرِ
٧ لِلشَّمْسِ غُرَّتُها لِلَّيْلِ طُرَّتُها * شَمْسٌ ولَيْلٌ مَعًا مِنْ أَعْجَبِ ٱلصُّوَرِ
٨ فَنَحْنُ بِٱللَّيْلِ فى ضَوْءِ ٱلنَّهارِ بِها * ونَحْنُ فى ٱلظُّهْرِ فى لَيْلٍ مِنَ الشَّعَرِ

٣ M. بى دليل ; M. ولا ذكرتهم . ٥ L. غزل . ٦ M. om. this verse.

XL

١ طَلَعَتْ بَيْنَ أَذْرِعاتٍ وبُصْرَى * بِنْتُ عَشْرٍ وأَرْبَعٍ لِى بَدْرا
٢ قَدْ تَعالَتْ عَلَى ٱلزَّمانِ جَلالًا * وتَسامَتْ عَلَيْهِ كِبْرًا وفَخْرا
٣ كُلُّ بَدْرٍ إذا تَناهَى كَمالًا * جاءَهُ نَقْصُهُ لِيُكْمِلَ شَهْرا
٤ غَيْرَ هٰذِى فَما لَها حَرَكاتٌ * فى بُرُوجٍ فَما تُشَفِّعُ وِتْرا
٥ حُقَّةٌ أُودِعَتْ عَبِيرًا ونَشْرًا * رَوْضَةٌ أَنْبَتَتْ رَبِيعًا وزَهْرا
٦ ٱنْتَهَى ٱلْحُسْنُ فِيكِ أَقْصَى مَداهُ * ما لِوُسْعِ ٱلْإمْكانِ مِثْلُكِ أُخْرَى

١ LM. ادرعات . ٤ M. هذه . ٦ M. بوسع .

XLI

١ رَعَى ٱللهُ طَيْرًا عَلَى بانَةٍ * قَدَ ٱفْصَحَ لى عَنْ صَحِيحِ ٱلْخَبَرْ
٢ بِأَنَّ ٱلْأَحِبَّةَ شَدُّوا عَلَى * رَواحِلِهِمْ ثُمَّ راحُوا سَحَرْ
٣ فَسِرْتُ وفى ٱلْقَلْبِ مِنْ أَجْلِهِمْ * جَحِيمٌ لِبَيْنِهِمُ تَسْتَعِرْ
٤ أُسابِقُهُمْ فى ظَلامِ ٱلدُّجَى * أُنادِى بِهِمْ ثُمَّ أَقْفُو ٱلْأَثَرْ
٥ وما لى دَلِيلٌ عَلَى إثْرِهِمْ * سِوَى نَفَسٍ مِنْ هَواهُمْ عَطِرْ
٦ رَفَعْنَ ٱلسِّجافَ أَضاءَ ٱلدُّجَى * فَسارَ ٱلرِّكابُ لِضَوْءِ ٱلْقَمَرْ

٣ L. يستعر . ٦ L. رفعن السحاب .

٧ فأرسلت دمعى أمام الركاب * فقالوا متى سال هذا النهر
٨ ولم يستطيعوا عبورا له * فقلت دموعى جرين درر
٩ كأن الرعود لِلَمع البروق * وسير الغمام لصوب المطر
١٠ وجيب القلوب لبرق الثغور * وسكب الدموع لركب نفر
١١ فيا من يشبه لين القدود * بلين القضيب الرطيب النضر
١٢ فلو عكس الأمر مثل الذى * فعلت لكان سليم النظر
١٣ فلين الغصون كلين القدود * وورد الرياض كورد الخفر

٨ L جرين دُرر ; M. جرت كالدرر . ٩ L. كصوب .
١٠ L. لنحو الثغور ; LM. كركب . ١١ LN. النظر .

XLII

١ يا أولى الألباب يا أهل النهى * همت ما بين المهاة والمها
٢ من سها عن السها فما سها * من سها عن المهاة قد سها
٣ سر به بسربه لسربه * فاللهى تفتح بالحمد اللهى
٤ إنها من فتيات عرب * من بنات الفرس أصلا إنها
٥ نظم الحسن من الدر لها * أشنبا أبيض صاف كالمها
٦ رابنى منها سفور راعنى * عنده منها جمال وبها
٧ فأنا ذو الموتتين منهما * هكذا القرآن قد جاء بها
٨ قلت ما بال سفور راعنى * موعد الأقوام إشراق المها
٩ قلت إنى فى حمى من فاجم * ساتر فلترسليه عندها
١٠ شعرنا هذا بلا قافية * إنما قصدى منه حرف ها
١١ غرضى لفظة ها من أجلها * لست أهوى البيع إلا ها وها

١ M. ياولى النهى . ٦ M. عندها منه ; L. جمالا . ٧ M. موتتين .
٨ M. الاقدم . ١١ M. لست ابتغ الا ها .

XLIII

١ وَلا أَنْسَ يَوْمًا عِنْدَ وانَةَ مَنْزِلِى * وَقَوْلى لِرَكْبٍ ظاعِنِينَ وَنُزَّلِ
٢ أَقِيمُوا عَلَيْنا ساعَةً نَشْتَفى بها * فإنّى وَمَنْ أَهْواهُمُ فى تَعَمُّلِ
٣ فإنْ رَحَلُوا ساروا بأَيْمَنِ طايِرٍ * وإنْ نَزَلُوا حَلُّوا بِأَخْصَبِ مَنْزِلِ
٤ وبِٱلشِّعْبِ مِنْ وادى قَناةٍ لَقِيتُهُمْ * وعَهْدى بِهِمْ بَيْنَ ٱلنَّقا وَٱلْمُشَلْشِلِ
٥ يُراعُونَ مَرْعَى ٱلْعِيسِ حَيْثُ وَجَدْنَهُ * ولَيْسَ يُراعوا قَلْبَ صَبٍّ مُضَلَّلِ
٦ فيا حادِىَ ٱلْأَجْمالِ رِفْقًا عَلَى فَتًى * تَراهُ لَدَى ٱلتَّوْديعِ كاسِرَ حَنْظَلِ
٧ يُخالِفُ بَيْنَ ٱلرّاحَتَيْنِ عَلَى ٱلْحَشا * يُسَكِّنُ قَلْبًا طارَ مِنْ حِرِّ مَحْمِلِ
٨ يَقولُونَ صَبْرًا وَٱلْأَسَى غَيْرُ صابِرٍ * فَما حِيلَتى وَٱلصَّبْرُ عَنّى بِمَعْزِلِ
٩ وَلَوْ كانَ لى صَبْرٌ وَكُنْتُ بِحُكْمِهِ * لَما صَبَرَتْ نَفْسى فَكَيْفَ وَلَيْسَ لى

١ L. ولم انس, so N. in marg.; L. راحلين ونزل; M. الرايحين; N. in marg. رايحين. ٩ LM. صبرا.

XLIV

١ طَلَعَ ٱلْبَدْرُ فى دُجَى ٱلشَّعَرِ * وَسَقَى ٱلْوَرْدَ نَرْجِسُ ٱلْحَوَرِ
٢ غادَةٌ تاهَتِ ٱلْحِسانُ بِها * وزَها نُورُها عَلَى ٱلْقَمَرِ
٣ إنْ سَرَتْ فى ٱلضَّميرِ يَجْرَحُها * ذٰلِكَ ٱلْوَهْمُ كَيْفَ بِٱلْبَصَرِ
٤ لُعْبَةٌ ذِكْرُنا يُذَوِّبُها * لَطُفَتْ عَنْ مَسارِحِ ٱلنَّظَرِ
٥ طَلَبَ ٱلنَّعْتُ أَنْ يُبَيِّنَها * فَتَعالَتْ فَعادَ ذا حَصَرِ
٦ وإذا رامَ أَنْ يُكَيِّفَها * لَمْ يَزَلْ ناكِصًا عَلَى ٱلْأَثَرِ
٧ إنْ أَراحَ ٱلْمَطِىَّ طالِبُها * لَمْ يُرِيحُوا مَطِيَّةَ ٱلْفِكَرِ
٨ رَوْحَةٌ كُلَّ مَنْ أُشِبَّ بِها * نَقَلَتْ عَنْ مَراتِبِ ٱلْبَشَرِ

٣ In LM. this verse is preceded by verses ١٠ and ١١.

٤ L. كعبة ذكرنا يطوف بها. ٨ L. رَوحت; M. روحنت; N. روحنة; L اشت بها; LMN. نقلته, which is *contra metrum*.

٩ غَيْرَةً أَنْ يُشابَ رايِقُها * بِٱلَّذى فى ٱلحِياضِ مِنْ كَدَرِ
١٠ هِىَ أَشْهَى مِنَ ٱلمَهاةِ سَنًا * صُورَةٌ لا تُقاسُ بِٱلصُّوَرِ
١١ فَلَكُ ٱلنُّورِ دُونَ أَخْمَصِها * تاجُها خارِجٌ عَنِ ٱلأُكَرِ

XLV

١ أَحْبابُ قَلْبى أَيْنَ هُمْ * بِٱللّٰهِ قُولُوا أَيْنَ هُمْ
٢ كَما رَأَيْتَ طَيْفَهُمْ * فَهَلْ تُرِينى عَيْنَهُمْ
٣ فَكَمْ وَكَمْ أَطْلُبُهُمْ * وَكَمْ سَأَلْتُ بَيْنَهُمْ
٤ حَتَّى أَمِنْتُ بَيْنَهُمْ * وَما أَمِنْتُ بَيْنَهُمْ
٥ لَعَلَّ سَعْدى حايِلٌ * بَيْنَ ٱلنَّوَى وَبَيْنَهُمْ
٦ لِتَنْعَمَ ٱلعَيْنُ بِهِمْ * فَلا أَقُولَ أَيْنَ هُمْ

١ LM. احبابنا. ٣ L. طلبتهم. ٥ L. بين الورى.

XLVI

١ بَيْنَ ٱلحَشا وَٱلعُيُونِ ٱلنُّجْلِ حَرْبُ هَوًى * وَٱلقَلْبُ مِنْ أَجْلِ ذاكَ ٱلحَرْبِ فى حَرَبِ
٢ لَمْياءَ لَعْساءَ مَعْسُولٌ مُقَبَّلُها * شَهادَةُ ٱلنَّحْلِ ما تَلْقَى مِنَ ٱلضَّرَبِ
٣ رَيّا ٱلمُخَلْخَلِ دَيْجُورٌ عَلَى قَمَرٍ * فى خَدِّها شَفَقٌ غُصْنٌ عَلَى كُثُبِ
٤ حَسْناءَ حالِيَةٌ لَيْسَتْ بِغانِيَةٍ * تَفْتَرُّ عَنْ بَرَدٍ ظَلْمٍ وَعَنْ شَنَبِ
٥ تَصُدُّ جِدًّا وَتَلْهُو بِٱلهَوَى لَعِبًا * وَٱلمَوْتُ ما بَيْنَ ذاكَ ٱلجِدِّ وَٱللَّعِبِ
٦ ما عَسْعَسَ ٱللَّيْلُ إِلّا جاءَ يَعْقُبُهُ * تَنَفُّسُ ٱلصُّبْحِ مَعْلُومٌ مِنَ ٱلحِقَبِ
٧ وَلا تَمُرُّ عَلَى رَوْضٍ رِياحُ صَبًا * تَحْوِى عَلَى كاعِباتٍ خُرَّدٍ عُرُبِ
٨ إِلّا أَمالَتْ وَنَمَّتْ فى تَنَسُّمِها * بِما حَمَلْنَ مِنَ ٱلأَزْهارِ وَٱلقُضُبِ
٩ سَأَلْتُ رِيحَ ٱلصَّبا عَنْهُمْ لِتُخْبِرَنى * قالَتْ وَما لَكَ فى ٱلأَخْبارِ مِنْ أَرَبِ
١٠ فى ٱلأَبْرَقَيْنِ وَفى بَرْكِ ٱلغِمادِ وَفى * بِرْكِ ٱلغَمِيمِ تَرَكْتُ ٱلحَجَّ عَنْ كَثَبِ

١ N. والعيون السود, but النجل in marg. ٥ M. تجد جدًا.

١٠ L. برك النعيم ; L. تركت الحى ; M. بركب الحى.

١١ لا تَستَقِرُّ بِهِمْ أَرْضٌ فقُلْتُ لَها * أَيْنَ ٱلمَفَرُّ وخَيْلُ ٱلشَّوْقِ فى ٱلطَّلَبِ

١٢ هَيْهاتَ لَيْسَ لَهُمْ مَغْنًى سِوَى خَلَدِى * فَحَيْثُ كُنْتُ يَكُونُ ٱلبَدْرُ فَٱرْتَقِبِ

١٣ أَلَيْسَ مَطْلَعُها وَهْىَ وَمَغْرِبُها * قَلْبى فقَدْ زالَ شُؤْمُ ٱلبانِ وٱلغَرَبِ

١٤ ما لِلْغُرابِ نَعِيقٌ فى مَنازِلِنا * وما لَهُ فى نِظامِ ٱلشَّمْلِ مِنْ نَدَبِ

١١ N. تستقلّ. ١٢ M. فحيث كانوا.

XLVII

١ حَمامَةَ ٱلبانِ بِذاتِ ٱلغَضَى * ضاقَ لِما حَمَّلْتِنِيهِ ٱلفَضا

٢ مَنْ ذا ٱلَّذى يَحْمِلُ شَجْوَ ٱلهَوَى * مَنْ ذا ٱلَّذى يَجْرَعُ مُرَّ ٱلقَضا

٣ أَقُولُ مِنْ وَجْدٍ ومِنْ لَوْعَةٍ * يا لَيْتَ مَنْ أَمْرَضَنى مَرَّضا

٤ مَرَّ بِبابِ ٱلدّارِ مُسْتَهْزِئًا * مُسْتَخْفِيًا مُعْتَجِرًا مُعْرِضا

٥ ما ضَرَّنى تَعْجِيرُهُ إِنَّما * أَضَرَّنى مِنْ كَوْنِهِ أَعْرَضا

٣ L. من وجدى ومن لوعتى.

XLVIII

١ يا حادِىَ ٱلعِيسِ بِسَلْعٍ عَرِّجِ * وَقِفْ عَلَى ٱلبانَةِ بِٱلْمُدَرَّجِ

٢ ونادِهِمْ مُسْتَعْطِفًا مُسْتَلْطِفًا * يا سادَتى هَلْ عِنْدَكُمْ مِنْ فَرَجِ

٣ بِرامَةٍ بَيْنَ ٱلنَّقا وحاجِرٍ * جارِيَةٌ مَقْصُورَةٌ فى هَوْدَجِ

٤ يا حُسْنَها مِنْ طَفْلَةٍ غُرَّتُها * تُضِىءُ لِلطّارِقِ مِثْلَ ٱلسُّرُجِ

٥ لُؤْلُؤَةٌ مَكْنُونَةٌ فى صَدَفٍ * مِنْ شَعَرٍ مِثْلِ سَوادِ ٱلسَّبَجِ

٦ لُؤْلُؤَةٌ غَوّاصُها ٱلفِكْرُ فما * يَنْفَكُّ فى أَغْوارِ تِلْكَ ٱللُّجَجِ

٧ يَحْسَبُها ناظِرُها ظَبْىَ نَقًا * مِنْ جِيدِها وحُسْنِ ذاكَ ٱلغَنَجِ

٨ كَأَنَّها شَمْسُ ضُحًى فى حَمَلٍ * قاطِعَةٌ أَقْصَى مَعالى ٱلدَّرَجِ

٩ إِنْ حَسَرَتْ بُرْقُعَها أَوْ سَفَرَتْ * أَزْرَتْ بِأَنْوارِ ٱلصَّباحِ ٱلأَبْلَجِ

٦ L. om. this verse. ٩ L. اسفرت ; M. الاملج.

١٠ نادَيْتُها بَيْنَ ٱلحِمَى ورامةٍ * مَنْ لِفَتًى حَلَّ بِسَلْعٍ يَرْتَجِى

١١ مَنْ لِفَتًى مُتَيَّمٍ فى مَهْمَهٍ * مُوَلَّهٍ مُدَلَّهِ ٱلعَقْلِ شَجِى

١٢ مَنْ لِفَتًى دَمْعُهُ مُغْرِقَةٌ * أَسْكَرَهُ خَمْرٌ بِذاكَ ٱلفَلَجِ

١٣ مَنْ لِفَتًى زَفْرَتُهُ مُحْرِقَةٌ * تَيَّمَهُ جَمالُ ذاكَ ٱلبَلَجِ

١٤ قَدْ لَعِبَتْ أَيْدِى ٱلهَوَى بِقَلْبِهِ * فما عَلَيْهِ فى ٱلّذى مِنْ حَرَجِ

١٠ L. حل . ١٣ L. om. this verse.

XLIX

١ مَنْ لى بِمَخْضُوبةِ ٱلبَنانِ * مَنْ لى بِمَعْسُولةِ ٱللِّسانِ

٢ مِنْ كاعِباتٍ ذَواتِ صَوْنٍ * نَواعِمٍ خُرَّدٍ حِسانِ

٣ بُدُورِ تَمٍّ عَلَى غُصُونٍ * هُنَّ مِنَ ٱلنَّقْصِ فى أَمانِ

٤ بِرَوْضةٍ مِنْ دِيارِ جِسْمِى * حَمامةٌ فَوْقَ غُصْنِ بانِ

٥ تَمُوتُ شَوْقًا تَذُوبُ عِشْقًا * لِما دَهاها ٱلّذى دَهانى

٦ تَنْدُبُ إِلْفًا تَذُمُّ دَهْرًا * رَماها قَصْدًا بِما رَمانى

٧ فِراقُ جارٍ ونَأْىُ دارٍ * فَيا زَمانى عَلَى زَمانى

٨ مَنْ لى بِمَنْ تَرْتَضى عَذابى * ما لى بِما تَرْتَضى يَدانِ

٥ M. لما دهانى . ٦ M. وقد رماها بما ; for the scansion of رماها cf. xviii, ٦.

L

١ وغادِرةٍ قد غادَرَتْ بِغَدائِرٍ * شَبِيهِ ٱلأَفاعِى مَنْ أَرادَ سَبِيلا

٢ سَلِيمًا وتَلْوِى لِينَها فتُذِيبُهُ * وتَتْرُكُهُ فَوْقَ ٱلفِراشِ عَلِيلا

٣ رَمَتْ بِسِهامِ ٱللَّحْظِ عَنْ قَوْسِ حاجِبٍ * فمِنْ أَيِّ شِقٍّ جِئْتُ كُنْتُ قَتِيلا

LI

١ بذاتِ ٱلأَضا وٱلمَأْزِمَيْنِ وبارِقٍ * وذى سَلَمٍ وٱلأَبْرَقَيْنِ لِطارِقِ

٢ بُرُوقُ سُيُوفٍ مِنْ بُرُوقِ مَباسِمٍ * نَوافِجِ مِسْكٍ ما أُبِيحَتْ لِناشِقِ

٣ فَإِنْ حُورِبُوا سَلُّوا سُيُوفَ لِحاظِهِمْ * وإِنْ سُولِمُوا هَدُّوا عُقُودَ ٱلْمَضايِقِ
٤ فنالُوا ونِلْنا لَذَّتَيْنِ تَساوَتا * فَمُلْكٌ لِمَعْشُوقٍ ومُلْكٌ لِعاشِقِ

٣ L. سيوف جفونهم . ٤ LMN. تساويا, but the commentary of N. had originally تساوتا ; L. فهاذى لمعشوق وتلك لعاشق .

LII

١ رَضِيتُ بِرَضْوَى رَوْضَةً ومُناخا * فَإِنَّ بِهِ مَرْعًى وفيهِ نُقاخا
٢ عَسَى أَهْلُ وُدّى يَسْمَعُونَ بِخِصْبِهِ * فَيَتَّخِذُوهُ مَرْبَعًا ومُناخا
٣ فَإِنَّ لَنا قَلْبًا بِهِنَّ مُعَلَّقًا * إِذا ما حَدا ٱلْحادِى بِهِنَّ أَناخا
٤ وإِنْ هُمْ تَنادَوْا لِلرَّحِيلِ وقَوَّزُوا * سَمِعْتَ لَهُ خَلْفَ ٱلرِّكابِ صُراخا
٥ فَإِنْ قَصَدُوا ٱلزَّوْرآءَ كانَ أَمامَهُمْ * وإِنْ يَمَّمُوا ٱلْجَرْعآءَ ثَمَّ أَناخا
٦ فما ٱلطَّيْرُ إِلَّا حَيْثُ كانُوا وخَيَّمُوا * فَإِنَّ لَهُ فى خَيِّهِنَّ فِراخا
٧ تُحارِبُ خَوْفٌ لى وخَوْفٌ مِنَ ٱجْلِها * وما واحِدٌ عَنْ قِرْنِهِ يَتَراخا
٨ إِذا خَطَفَتْ أَبْصارَنا سُبُحاتُها * أَصَمَّ لَها صَوْتُ ٱلشَّهِيقِ صِماخا

٦ L. فى خيمهن . ٧ L. يحارب ; L. عن حبه .

LIII

١ إِذا ما ٱلْتَقَيْنا لِلْوَداعِ حَسِبْتَنا * لَدَى ٱلضَّمِّ وٱلتَّعْنِيقِ حَرْفًا مُشَدَّدا
٢ فَنَحْنُ وإِنْ كُنّا مُثَنًّى شُخُوصُنا * فما تَنْظُرُ ٱلْأَبْصارُ إِلَّا مُوَحَّدا
٣ وما ذاكَ إِلَّا مِنْ نُحُولى ونُورِهِ * فَلَوْلا أَنِينى ما رَأَتْ لِىَ مَشْهَدا

٢ L. وان كانت ; LM. فما تبصر .

LIV

١ وقالُوا ٱلشُّمُوسُ بِدارِ ٱلْفَلَكْ * وهَلْ مَنْزِلُ ٱلشَّمْسِ إِلَّا ٱلْفَلَكْ
٢ إِذا قامَ عَرْشٌ عَلَى ساقِهِ * فَلَمْ يَبْقَ إِلَّا ٱسْتِوآءُ ٱلْمَلِكْ
٣ إِذا خَلَصَ ٱلْقَلْبُ مِنْ جَبْلِهِ * فما هُوَ إِلَّا نُزُولُ ٱلْمَلَكْ

٢ L. فلم يبق الا نزول الملك . ٣ LM. اخلص .

٤ تَمَلَّكَنِى وتَمَلَّكْتُهُ * فَكُلٌّ لِصاحِبِهِ قَدْ مَلَكْ

٥ فكَوْنِى مِلْكًا لَهُ بَيِّنٌ * ومِلْكِى لَهُ قَوْلُهُ هَيْتَ لَكْ

٦ فيا حادِىَ ٱلعِيسِ عَرِّجْ بنا * ولا تَعْدُ بِٱلرَّكْبِ دارَ ٱلفَلَكْ

٧ أَعَلَّكَ دارٌ عَلَى شاطِئٍ * بِقُرْبِ ٱلمُسَنَّى وما عَلَّلَكْ

٨ فَلَيْتَ ٱلَّذِى بِى وحُمِّلْتُهُ * مِنَ ٱلحُبِّ رَبُّ ٱلهَوَى حَمَّلَكْ

٩ فَلَيْسَ زَرُودٌ ولا حاجِرٌ * ولا سَلْمُ مَنْزِلًا أَنْحَلَكْ

١٠ ظَلِلْتَ لِبَحْرِ ٱلنَّوَى طالِبًا * سَحابَ ٱلوِصالِ وما ظَلَّلَكْ

١١ أَذَلَّكَ عِزٌّ لِسُلْطانِهِ * فَلَيْتَ كما ذَلَّكَ ذَلَّ لَكْ

١٢ ويا لَيْتَهُ إِذْ أَبَى عِزَّةً * تَذَلَّلَهُ لَيْتَهُ ذَلَّلَكْ

٨ L. رب السما. ٩ LMN. منزل. ١٠ M. بحر الهوى. ١١ L. كما ذللك ذل لك; M. اذل لك كما ذللك. ١٢ M. ذللك.

LV

١ أَغِيبُ فَيُفْنِى ٱلشَّوْقُ نَفْسِى فَأَلْتَقِى * فلا أَشْتَفِى فَٱلشَّوْقُ غَيْبًا ومَحْضَرا

٢ ويُحْدِثُ لِى لُقْياهُ ما لَمْ أَظُنَّهُ * وكانَ ٱلشِّفا داءً مِنَ ٱلوَجْدِ آخَرا

٣ لِأَنِّى أَرَى شَخْصًا يَزِيدُ جَمالُهُ * إذا ما ٱلتَقَيْنا نَضْرَةً وتَكَبُّرا

٤ فلا بُدَّ مِنْ وَجْدٍ يَكُونُ مُقارِنًا * لِما زادَ مِنْ حُسْنٍ نِظامًا مُحَرَّرا

٢ L. مكان الشفى. ٣ LN. نظرة.

LVI

١ أَلْقَصْرُ ذو ٱلشُّرُفاتِ مِنْ بَغْدادِ * لا ٱلقَصْرُ ذو ٱلشُّرُفاتِ مِنْ سِنْدادِ

٢ وٱلتاجُ مِنْ فَوْقِ ٱلرِّياضِ كَأَنَّهُ * عَذْراءُ قَدْ جُلِيَتْ بِأَعْطَرِ نادِ

٣ ٱلرِّيحُ تَلْعَبُ بِٱلغُصُونِ فَتَنْثَنِى * فَكَأَنَّهُ مِنْها عَلَى مِيعادِ

٤ وكَأَنَّ دِجْلَةَ سِلْكُها فى جِيدِها * وٱلبَعْلَ سَيِّدُنا ٱلإِمامُ ٱلهادِى

٥ ٱلنّاصِرُ ٱلمَنْصُورُ خَيْرُ خَلِيفَةٍ * لا يَمْتَطِى فى ٱلحَرْبِ مَتْنَ جَوادِ

١ N. من شداد. ٥ LM. خليقة.

٦ صَلَّى عَلَيْهِ ٱللّٰهُ ما صَدَحَتْ بِهِ * وَرْقا مُطَوَّقَةٌ عَلَى مَيّادِ
٧ وكَذاكَ ما بَرَقَتْ بُرُوقُ مَباسِمٍ * سَحَّتْ لَنا مِنْ مُقْلَتَىَّ غَوادِ
٨ مِنْ خُرَّدٍ كَٱلشَّمْسِ أَقْلَعَ غَيْمُها * فَبَدَتْ بِأَنْوَرِ مُسْتَنِيرٍ بادِ

LVII

١ أَلا يا نَسِيمَ ٱلرِّيحِ بَلِّغْ مَها نَجْدِ * بِأَنّى عَلَى ما تَعْلَمُونَ مِنَ ٱلْعَهْدِ
٢ وقُلْ لِفَتاةِ ٱلْحَيِّ مَوْعِدُنا ٱلْحِمَى * غُدَيَّةَ يَوْمِ ٱلسَّبْتِ عِنْدَ رُبا نَجْدِ
٣ عَلَى ٱلرَّبْوَةِ ٱلْحَمْراءِ مِنْ جانِبِ ٱلصُّوَى * وعَنْ أَيْمَنِ ٱلْأَفْلاجِ وٱلْعَلَمِ ٱلْفَرْدِ
٤ فإِنْ كانَ حَقًّا ما تَقُولُ وعِنْدَها * إِلَيَّ مِنَ ٱلشَّوْقِ ٱلْمُبَرِّحِ ما عِنْدى
٥ إِلَيْها ففى حَرِّ ٱلظَّهِيرَةِ نَلْتَقى * بِخَيْمَتِها سِرًّا عَلَى أَصْدَقِ ٱلْوَعْدِ
٦ فنُلْقِى ونُلْقِى ما نُلاقِى مِنَ ٱلْهَوَى * ومِنْ شِدَّةِ ٱلْبَلْوَى ومِنْ أَلَمِ ٱلْوَجْدِ
٧ أَأَضْغاثُ أَحْلامٍ أَبُشْرَى مَنامَةٍ * أَنُطْقُ زَمانٍ كانَ فى نُطْقِهِ سَعْدى
٨ لَعَلَّ ٱلَّذى ساقَ ٱلْأَمانى يَسُوقُها * عِيانًا فيُهْدِى رَوْضُها لى جَنَى ٱلْوَرْدِ

١ LM. يعلمون . ٣ LM. الافلاح .

LVIII

١ أَلا هَلْ إِلَى ٱلزُّهْرِ ٱلْحِسانِ سَبِيلُ * وهَلْ لى عَلَى آثارِهِنَّ دَلِيلُ
٢ وهَلْ لى بِخَيْماتِ ٱللِّوَى مِنْ مُعَرَّسٍ * وهَلْ لِيَ فى ظِلِّ ٱلْأَراكِ مَقِيلُ
٣ فقالَ لِسانُ ٱلْحالِ يُخْبِرُ أَنَّها * تَقُولُ تَمَنَّ ما إِلَيْهِ سَبِيلُ
٤ وِدادى صَحِيحٌ فيكَ يا غايَةَ ٱلْمُنَى * وقَلْبِىَ مِنْ ذاكَ ٱلْوِدادِ عَلِيلُ
٥ تَعالَيْتَ مِنْ بَدْرٍ عَلَى ٱلْقَلْبِ طالِعٍ * ولَيْسَ لَهُ بَعْدَ ٱلطُّلُوعِ أُفُولُ
٦ فَدَيْتُكَ يا مَنْ عَزَّ حُسْنًا ونَخْوَةً * فلَيْسَ لَهُ بَيْنَ ٱلْحِسانِ عَدِيلُ
٧ فرَوْضُكَ مَطْلُولٌ ووَرْدُكَ يانِعٌ * وحُسْنُكَ مَعْشُوقٌ عَلَيْهِ قَبُولُ
٨ وزَهْرُكَ بَسّامٌ وغُصْنُكَ ناعِمٌ * تَمِيلُ لَهُ ٱلْأَرْواحُ حَيْثُ يَمِيلُ
٩ وظَرْفُكَ فَتّانٌ وطَرْفُكَ صارِمٌ * بِهِ فارِسُ ٱلْبَلْوَى عَلَىَّ يَصُولُ

٣ LM. تمنى ; L. ما عليك سبيل .

LIX

١ لِطَيْبَةَ ظَبْيٌ صارِمٌ * مُجَرَّدٌ مِنْ طَرْفِها ٱلسّاحِرِ
٢ وفى عَرَفاتٍ عَرَفْتُ ٱلّذى * تُرِيدُ فلَمْ أَكُ بِٱلصّابِرِ
٣ ولَيْلَةَ جَمْعٍ جَمَعْنا بِها * كَما جآءَ فى ٱلْمَثَلِ ٱلسّايِرِ
٤ يَمِينُ ٱلْفَتاةِ يَمِينٌ فلا * تَكُنْ تَطْمَئِنُّ إلى غادِرِ
٥ مُنًى بِمِنًى نِلْتُها لَيْتَها * تَدُومُ إلى ٱلزَّمَنِ ٱلآخِرِ
٦ تَوَلَّعْتُ فى لَعْلَعٍ بِٱلّتى * تُرِيكَ سَنا ٱلْقَمَرِ ٱلزّاهِرِ
٧ رَمَتْ رامةً وعَبَتْ بِٱلصَّبا * وحَجَّرَتِ ٱلْحَجْرَ بِٱلحاجِرِ
٨ وشامَتْ بُرَيْقًا على بارِقٍ * بِأَسْرَعَ مِنْ خَطْرَةِ ٱلْخاطِرِ
٩ وغاضَتْ مِياهُ ٱلْغَضا مِنْ غَضًى * بِأَضْلُعِهِ مِنْ هَوًى ساجِرِ
١٠ وبانَتْ بِبانِ ٱلنَّقا فٱنْتَقَتْ * لآلِئَ مَكْنُونِهِ ٱلْفاخِرِ
١١ وآضَتْ بِذاتِ ٱلأَضى ٱلْقَهْقَرَى * حِذارًا مِنَ ٱلأَسَدِ ٱلْخادِرِ
١٢ بِذى سَلَمٍ أَسْلَمَتْ مُهْجَتى * إلى لَحْظِها ٱلفاتِكِ ٱلْفاتِرِ
١٣ حَمَتْ بِٱلْحِمَى ولَوَتْ بِٱللِّوَى * لِعَطْفَةِ جارِحِها ٱلْكاسِرِ
١٤ وفى عالِجٍ عالَجَتْ أَمْرَها * لِتُفْلِتَ مِنْ مِخْلَبِ ٱلطّايِرِ
١٥ خَوَرْنَقُها خارِقٌ لِلسَّمآءِ * يَسْمُو ٱعْتِلآءً على ٱلنّاظِرِ

٩ LM. ساحر . ١٢ L. الى جعدها . ١٣ N. كعطفة . ١٥ L. ويسمو .

LX

١ أَلْمِمْ بِمَنْزِلِ أَحْبابٍ لَهُمْ ذِمَمُ * سَحَّتْ عَلَيْهِ سَحابٌ صَوْبُها دِيَمُ
٢ وٱسْتَنْشِقِ ٱلرِّيحَ مِنْ تِلْقآءِ أَرْضِهِمِ * شَوْقًا لِتُخْبِرَكَ ٱلأَرْواحُ أَيْنَ هُمُ
٣ أَظُنُّهُمْ خَيَّمُوا بِٱلْبانِ مِنْ إِضَمٍ * حَيْثُ ٱلْعَرارُ وحَيْثُ ٱلشِّيحُ وٱلْكَتَمُ

١ M. دمم .

LXI

١ أَلَا يا بانةَ ٱلوادى * بِشاطِى نَهْرِ بَغْدادِ
٢ شَجانى فيكِ نَوّاحٌ * طَرُوبٌ فَوْقَ مَيّادِ
٣ يُذَكِّرُنى تَرَنُّمُهُ * تَرَنُّمَ رَبّةِ ٱلسّادى
٤ إذا سَوَّتْ مَثالِثَها * فَلا تَذْكُرْ أخا ٱلْهادى
٥ وإنْ جادَتْ بِنَغْمَتِها * فَمَنْ أَنْجَشَةُ ٱلْحادى
٦ بِذى ٱلخَضِماتِ مِنْ سَلْمَى * يَمِينًا ثُمَّ سِنْدادِ
٧ لَقَدْ أَصْبَحْتُ مَشْغُوفًا * بِمَنْ سَكَنَتْ بِأَجْيادِ
٨ غَلِطْنا إنّما سَكَنَتْ * سُوَيْدا خِلْبِ أَكْبادى
٩ لَقَدْ تاهَ ٱلْجَمالُ بِها * وفاحَ ٱلْمِسْكُ وٱلْجادى

٢ L. فيكِ صياحٌ ; M. يناح ; N. originally نواح, altered to نمام ; in marg. مناح.   ٦ N. شدّاد.

قال المؤلّف رحمه الله ونفعنا به والمسلمين اجمعين آمين قد كان السبب فى شرحى لهذا الديوان ترجمان الاشواق الذى انشأته بمكّة شرّفها الله تعالى وعظّمها سؤال صاحبى المسعود ابى محمد بدر بن عبد الله الحبشى الخادم وسؤال الولد البارّ شمس الدين اسماعيل بن سودكين النورى بمدينة حلب وقد سمع من بعض الفقها قولًا انكره وهو انّه سمعه يقول قول الشيخ فى اوّل هذا الترجمان انّه قصد بما فيه من الابيات الغزلية علومًا واسرارًا وحقايق ليس بصحيح والله اعلم وانّما فعله الشيخ تستّرًا حتّى لا ينسب اليه لسان الغزل مع ما هو عليه من الدين والصلاح فذكر ذلك لنا الولد شمس الدين اسمعيل فشرعت فى شرحه بحلب وحضر سماع بعضه ذلك الفقيه المتكلّم وجملة من الفقها بقراءة كمال الدين ابى القاسم ابن

نجم الدين القاضى ابن العديم بمنزلنا وفّقه الله تعالى واعجلنا السفر فأتممناه بالتقصير والعجز فى التأريخ المذكور ولمّا سمعه ذلك القايل قال لشمس الدين اسمعيل ما بقيت بعد هذا الامر اتّهم احدًا من اهل هذه الطريقة فيما يتكلّمون به من الكلام المعتاد ويزعمون انهم يشيرون به الى علوم اصطلحوا عليها بهذه الالفاظ وحسن ظنّه فانتفع فهذا كان سبب شرحى لهذا الترجمان ولله الحمد والمنّة وبه الحول والقوّة من الزايد والناقص.

TRANSLATION AND COMMENTARY

I

1. Would that I were aware whether they knew what heart they possessed!
2. And would that my heart knew what mountain-pass they threaded!
3. Dost thou deem them safe or dost thou deem them dead?
4. Lovers lose their way in love and become entangled.

Commentary

1. 'They,' i.e. the Divine Ideas (المناظر العُلَى), of which the hearts (of gnostics) are passionately enamoured, and by which the spirits are distraught, and for whose sake the godly workers (العمّال الالاهيون) perform their works of devotion.

'What heart': he refers to the perfect Muḥammadan heart, because it is not limited by stations (المقامات). Nevertheless, it is possessed by the Divine Ideas, for they seek it and it seeks them. They cannot know that they possess it, for they belong to its essence, inasmuch as it beholds in them nothing except its own nature.

2. 'What mountain-pass they threaded,' i.e. what gnostic's heart they entered when they vanished from mine. 'Mountain-pass' signifies a 'station' (مقام), which is fixed, in contrast to a 'state' (حال), which is fleeting.

3. The Divine Ideas, *quâ* Ideas, exist only in the existence of the seer; they are 'dead' in so far as the seer is non-existent.

4. Lovers are perplexed between two opposite things, for the lover wishes to be in accord with the Beloved and also wishes to be united with Him, so that if the Beloved wishes to be separated from the lover, the lover is in a dilemma.

II

1. On the day of parting they did not saddle the full-grown reddish-white camels until they had mounted the peacocks upon them,
2. Peacocks with murderous glances and sovereign power: thou wouldst fancy that each of them was a Bilqís on her throne of pearls.
3. When she walks on the glass pavement[1] thou seest a sun on a celestial sphere in the bosom of Idrís.
4. When she kills with her glances, her speech restores to life, as tho' she, in giving life thereby, were Jesus.
5. The smooth surface of her legs is (like) the Tora in brightness, and I follow it and tread in its footsteps as tho' I were Moses.
6. She is a bishopess, one of the daughters of Rome, unadorned: thou seest in her a radiant Goodness.[2]
7. Wild is she, none can make her his friend; she has gotten in her solitary chamber a mausoleum for remembrance.
8. She has baffled everyone who is learned in our religion, every student of the Psalms of David, every Jewish doctor, and every Christian priest.
9. If with a gesture she demands the Gospel, thou wouldst deem us to be priests and patriarchs and deacons.
10. The day when they departed on the road, I prepared for war the armies of my patience, host after host.
11. When my soul reached the throat (i.e. when I was at the point of death), I besought that Beauty and that Grace to grant me relief,
12. And she yielded—may God preserve us from her evil, and may the victorious king repel Iblís!
13. I exclaimed, when her she-camel set out to depart, 'O driver of the reddish-white camels, do not drive them away with her!'

[1] Kor. xxvii, 44.

[2] The author explains that ناموس is equivalent to خَيِّر.

E

Commentary

1. 'The full-grown camels,' i.e. the actions inward and outward, for they exalt the good word to Him who is throned on high, as He hath said: '*And the good deed exalts it*' (Kor. xxxv, 11). 'The peacocks' mounted on them are his loved ones: he likens them to peacocks because of their beauty. The peacocks are the spirits of those actions, for no action is acceptable or good or fair until it hath a spirit consisting in the intention or desire of its doer. He compares them to birds inasmuch as they are spiritual and also for the variety of their beauty.

2. 'With murderous glances and sovereign power': he refers to the Divine wisdom (حكمة الاهية) which accrues to a man in his hours of solitude, and which assaults him with such violence that he is unable to behold his personality (فتكه عن مشاهدة ذاته), and which exercises dominion over him.

'A Bilqís on her throne of pearls': he refers to that which was manifested to Gabriel and to the Prophet during his night journey upon the bed (رَفْرَف) of pearl and jacinth in the terrestrial heaven, when Gabriel alone swooned by reason of his knowledge of Him who manifested Himself on that occasion. The author calls the Divine wisdom 'Bilqís' on account of its being the child of theory, which is subtle, and practice, which is gross, just as Bilqís was both spirit and woman, since her father was of the Jinn and her mother was of mankind.

3. The mention of Idrís alludes to her lofty and exalted rank. 'In the bosom of Idrís,' i.e. under his control, in respect of his turning her wheresoever he will, as the Prophet said: 'Do not bestow wisdom on those who are unworthy of it, lest ye do it a wrong.' The opposite case is that of one who speaks because he is dominated by his feeling (حال), and who is therefore under the control of an influence (وارد). In this verse the author calls attention to his puissance in virtue of a prophetic heritage (على تمكنه

(ميراثا نبويًّا), for the prophets are masters of their spiritual feelings (احوال), whereas most of the saints are mastered by them. The sun is joined to Idrís because the sun is his sphere, and the Divine wisdom is described as 'walking' (instead of 'running', etc.) because of her pride and haughtiness, and because she moves in the feelings of this heart and changes from one feeling to another with a sort of absolute power (بضربٍ من التمكّن).

4. 'She kills with her glances': referring to the station of passing away in contemplation (الفناء فى المشاهدة). 'Her speech restores to life': referring to the completion of the moulding of man when the spirit was breathed into him. She is compared to Jesus in reference to Kor. xxxviii, 72, '*And I breathed into him of My spirit*,' or Kor. xvi, 42, '*That We say to it "Be", and it is*.'

5. 'Her legs': referring to Bilqís and the glass pavement (Kor. xxvii, 44).

'Is like the Tora in brightness,' because the Tora (التوراة) is derived from the phrase وَرَى الزَّنْد, 'the stick produced fire.' The four faces (اوجه) of the Tora, namely, the four Books (the Koran, the Psalms, the Pentateuch, and the Gospel), correspond to the fourfold light mentioned in Kor. xxiv, 35 (المشكاة والمصباح والزجاجة والزيت).

6. 'One of the daughters of Rome': this wisdom, being of the race of Jesus (عيسويّة المَحْتِد), is described as belonging to the Roman Empire. 'Unadorned,' i.e. she is of the essence of unification (التوحيد) and without any vestige of adornment from the Divine Names, yet there shines from her the 'radiance' of Absolute Goodness, viz. the burning splendours (السُبُحات المُحْرِقة) which, if God were to remove the veils of light and darkness, would consume the glories of His face (سُبُحات وجهه).

7. 'Wild is she, none can make her his friend,' because contemplation of the Essence is a passing away (فنآء), in

which, as as-Sayyárí[1] said, there is no pleasure. She is 'wild', inasmuch as noble souls desire to seize her, but she does not show friendship to them, because no relation exists between them and her.

'In her solitary chamber,' i.e. in the heart. Her solitude is her looking on herself, for God says, 'Neither My earth nor My heaven contains Me, but I am contained by the heart of My servant who is a believer'; and since the heart which contains this essential wisdom of the race of Jesus is bare and empty of all attributes (فى مقام التجريد والتنزيه), it is like a desert and she is like a wild animal. Then he mentions the marble tomb of the Roman emperors, that such a mausoleum may remind her of death, which is the severance of union, and make her shun familiarity with the created world on account of this severance.

8. The four Books (the Koran, the Psalms, the Tora, and the Gospel) are here indicated by the mention of those who study and expound them. All the sciences comprised in the four Books point only to the Divine Names and are incapable of solving a question that concerns the Divine Essence.

9. If this spiritual being, forasmuch as she is of the race of Jesus, appeals to the Gospel by way of justifying it in anything which men's thoughts have falsely imputed to it, we humble ourselves before her and serve her no less devotedly than do the heads of the Church, because of her majesty and sovereign might.

10. 'Upon the road,' i.e. the spiritual ascension (المعراج الروحانى).

11. 'To grant me relief': he means what the Prophet meant by his saying, 'Lo, the breath of the Merciful comes to me from the quarter of al-Yaman.' The writer begs that the world of breaths (عالم الانفاس) may continually be wafted from her to him along with the spiritual feelings (احوال).

[1] Abu 'l-'Abbás as-Sayyárí of Merv (died 342 A.H.). His doctrine of union and separation (جمع و تفرقة) is explained by al-Hujwírí in the *Kashf al-Mahjúb.*

The Arabs refer to this in their poetry, for they speak of giving greetings and news to be delivered by the winds when they blow.

12. 'May God preserve us from her evil!' He refers to the Tradition 'I take refuge with Thee from Thyself'.

'The victorious king,' i.e. thoughts of knowledge and Divine guidance.

'Iblís,' i.e. the thought of becoming one with God (اتّحاد), for this is a hard station, and few who attain to it escape from the doctrines of اتّحاد and incarnation (حُلول). It is the station indicated in the Tradition 'I am his ear and his eye', etc.

13. He says, 'When this spiritual essence desired to quit this noble heart on account of its (the heart's) return from the station denoted by the words, "I have an hour which I share with none save my Lord," to the task imposed upon it of presiding over the phenomenal worlds, for which purpose its gaze is directed towards the Divine Names, the lofty aspiration (همّة) on which this spiritual essence was borne to the heart, took its departure.' He calls this aspiration 'her she-camel', and the drivers of such aspirations are the angels who approach nearest to God (المقرّبون).

III

1. O my two friends, pass by al-Kathíb and turn towards La'la' and seek the waters of Yalamlam,
2. For there dwell those whom thou knowest and those to whom belong my fasting and my pilgrimage and my visit to the holy places and my festival.
3. Never let me forget at al-Muḥaṣṣab of Miná and at al-Manḥar al-A'lá and Zamzam certain grave matters.
4. Their Muḥaṣṣab is my heart, because of their casting the pebbles, and their place of sacrifice is my soul, and their well is my blood.
5. O camel-driver, if thou comest to Ḥájir, stop the beasts a little while and give a greeting,

6. And address to the red tents on the side of the guarded pasture the salutation of one who longs for you and is distraught.
7. And if they return thy greeting, once more let the East wind bring thy salaam to them ; and if they are silent, journey on with thy camels and advance
8. To the river of Jesus, where their riding-camels halted and where the white tents lie beside the river-mouth,
9. And call Da'd and ar-Rabáb and Zaynab and Hind and Salmá and Lubná, and listen,
10. And ask them whether at al-Ḥalba is She, the limber one who shows thee the radiance of the sun when she smiles.

Commentary

1. 'O my two friends,' i.e. his reason and his faith.

'Al-Kathíb,' the place of contemplation.

'La'la',' the place of bewilderment and amazement, that he may no more be conscious of love and longing.

'The waters of Yalamlam,' i.e. the fountain of life, since water is the source of every living thing.

2. 'Thou knowest': he addresses Faith, not Reason, for knowledge of the Essence and of its attributes is gained solely by means of Faith.

'And those to whom belong,' etc., i.e. the Divine attributes.

'My fasting': he means the quality of being independent of food (الصفة الصَّمَدانية), as God said, 'Fasting belongs to Me,' i.e. that quality cannot truly be predicated of a man; yet a man has some part in fasting, since it entails abstinence from food and nourishment.

'My pilgrimage,' i.e. a repeated turning towards this pure Essence for the sake of gaining a blessing at every moment from the Divine Names. This pilgrimage and visitation (اعتمار) is incessant, though a man is momently going from one Name to another.

'My festival,' referring to the concentration (جَمْع) of the mind when all mystical stations and Divine verities are united therein, just as all sorts and conditions of men assemble at Mecca for one purpose.

3. 'Never let me forget': he alludes to an occasion when he became invested with Divine qualities (تخلّقاً الاهيّا) in the sense of the Tradition 'I am his ear and his eye', and he also calls attention to his having attained by Divine investiture the station which is described in the words '*And thy Lord is not forgetful*' (Kor. xix, 65).

'At al-Muḥaṣṣab,' the place where the pebbles are cast. He refers to the verse '*And remember God even as ye remember your fathers, or more reverently*' (Kor. ii, 196), i.e. in this place cast the memory of your fathers out of your hearts and mouths.

'At al-Manḥar al-A'lá,' the place of (spiritual) sacrifice, as the poet says:

'Thou offerest victims, but I offer my life-blood.'

'Zamzam': he means the station of everlasting life.

4. 'Their Muḥaṣṣab': 'their' refers to the Divine verities which descend upon the heart and cast out sensual and devilish thoughts.

'Their place of sacrifice': the story is well known of the youth who mentally offered himself at Miná when he saw the people offering sacrifice, and died on the spot.

5. 'O camel-driver': he addresses the Desire which drives his thoughts to the abode of those whom he loves.

'Ḥájir': *ḥijr* is the understanding, and the way (to God) is only through faith and contemplation, not through the understanding in respect of its power of reflection but in virtue of its cognition and belief.

'Stop the beasts a little while,' because when the lover first approaches the dwelling-place of his beloved he is dazed and dumbfounded and often swoons; consequently he is apt to break the rules of good manners in greeting her.

6. 'The red tents': the Arabs deem red the most beautiful of all colours, and red tents are reserved for brides.

'On the side of the guarded pasture,' i.e. the tents are

inaccessible except to those who have the right to approach them. He calls the tents *qibáb* (round tents or domes) because roundness is the first and best of shapes, and he says that the Divine Realities which he loves are in their original home, which is beside God, not beside any phenomenal object, for they belong to 'the world of command' (عالم الأمْر).

7. 'Let the East wind,' etc.: he mentions the East wind particularly, because *ṣabá* signifies 'inclination' (*mayl*).

8. 'To the river of Jesus,' i.e. to the ample knowledge manifested in Jesus (العلم المتّسع العيسوىّ المَشْهَد).

'The white tents': white, because Jesus was born of a virgin.

'Beside the river-mouth,' i.e. this knowledge is approached by the way of Divine allocution and manifestation (من حيث اللسن والفبوانية).

9. He says, 'Call the names of these Divine Realities according to their difference, in order that whichever is yours may respond to you and that thus you may know what is your position in regard to them.'

10. 'Al-Ḥalba,' a quarter of Baghdád. *Ḥalba* means 'racecourse'. The Divine Realities strive to outstrip one another in haste to reach the phenomena which display their traces and manifest their power. Hence he speaks of 'the limber one', i.e. inclining towards the phenomenal world.

'The radiance of the sun': formerly thou wert in a station of Jesus, but now thou art asking of a station of Idrís, lofty and polar (علوىّ قُطبى), for to him belongs the fourth heaven.

'When she smiles': he indicates that this is the station of Expansion (مقام البَسْط) and that she is with him in joy and beauty (not in awe and majesty).

IV

1. Greeting to Salmá and to those who dwell in the preserve, for it behoves one who loves tenderly like me to give greeting.

2. And what harm to her if she gave me a greeting in return? But fair women are subject to no authority.
3. They journeyed when the darkness of night had let down its curtains, and I said to her, 'Pity a passionate lover, outcast and distraught,
4. Whom desires eagerly encompass and at whom speeding arrows are aimed wheresoever he bends his course.'
5. She displayed her front-teeth and a levin flashed, and I knew not which of the twain rent the gloom,
6. And she said, 'Is it not enough for him that I am in his heart and that he beholds me at every moment? Is it not enough?'

COMMENTARY

1. 'Salmá': he alludes to a Solomonic ecstasy (حالة سليمانية), which descended upon him from the station of Solomon in virtue of a prophetic heritage.

'In the preserve,' i.e. an unattainable station, viz. prophecy, whereof the gate was closed by Muḥammad, the last of the prophets. Solomon's experience of this Divine wisdom (حكمة) in so far as he was a prophet is different from his experience of it in so far as he was a saint, and we share it with him only in the latter case, since our experience of it is derived from the saintship which is the greatest circle (الدائرة العُظمى).

2. God does nothing of necessity: whatever comes to us from Him is by His favour. The author indicates this Divine Solomonic apparition (*nukta*) by the term 'marble statues' (i.e. women fair as marble statues). He means that she does not answer by speech, for if she did so her speech would be other than her essence, whereas her essence is single, so that her advent is identical with her speech and with her visible presence and with her hearing; and in this respect all the Divine Realities and Attributes resemble her.

3. 'They journeyed,' etc.: the ascension of the prophets always took place during the night, because night is the time of mystery and concealment.

'The darkness of night,' i.e. the veil of the Unseen let down the curtains of gross corporeal existence, which is the night of this animal organism, throwing a shroud over the spiritual subtleties and noble sciences which it enshrines. These, however, are not to be reached except by journeying through bodily actions and sensual thoughts, and whilst a man is thus occupied the Divine wisdom goes away from his heart, so that on his return he finds her gone and follows her with his aspiration.

4. 'Speeding arrows': he describes this celestial form as shooting his heart, wherever it turns, with the arrows of her glances, as God said, '*Wheresoever ye turn, there is the face of Allah*' (Kor. ii, 109).

5. 'She displayed her front-teeth,' etc., i.e. this lover found his whole being illuminated, for '*God is the light of the heavens and the earth*' (Kor. xxiv, 35), and the Prophet also said in his prayer, 'O God, put a light into my ear and into my eye,' and after mentioning the different members of his body he concluded, 'and make the whole of me one light,' viz. by the manifestation of Thy essence. Such a manifestation is compared to a flash of lightning on account of its not continuing. The author says that he did not know whether his being was illuminated by the manifestation proceeding from this Divine wisdom, which smiled upon him, or by a simultaneous manifestation of the Divine Essence.

6. 'She said,' etc., i.e. let him not seek me from without and let it satisfy him that I have descended into his heart, so that he beholds me in his essence and through his essence at every moment.

V

1. My longing sought the Upland and my affliction the Lowland, so that I was between Najd and Tiháma.
2. They are two contraries which cannot meet: hence my disunion will never be repaired.
3. What am I to do? What shall I devise? Guide me O my censor, do not affright me with blame!

4. Sighs have risen aloft and tears are pouring over my cheeks.
5. The camels, footsore from the journey, long for their homes and utter the plaintive cry of the frenzied lover.
6. After they have gone, my life is naught but annihilation. Farewell to it and to patience!

COMMENTARY

1. 'The Upland,' referring to God on His throne.

2. 'They are two contraries,' etc.: he says, 'Inasmuch as the spiritual element in man is always governing the body, it can never contemplate that which is uncomposed apart from its body and independently, as some Ṣúfís and philosophers and ignorant persons declare.' Hence the writer says, 'my disunion will never be repaired,' i.e., 'I cannot become united with Him who is pure and simple, and who resembles my essence and reality. Therefore longing is folly, for this station is unattainable, but longing is a necessary attribute of love, and accordingly I cease not from longing.'

3. 'My censor,' i.e. the blaming soul (النفس اللوّامة).

5. 'The camels,' i.e. the actions or the lofty thoughts (الهِمَم)—since, in my opinion, such thoughts belong to the class of actions—on which the good words (الكَلِم الطيب) mount to the throne of God. They 'long for their homes', i.e. for the Divine Names from which they proceeded and by which they are controlled.

6. 'My life is naught but annihilation': he says, 'When the lofty thoughts ascend to their goal I remain in the state of passing away from passing away (الفناء عن الفناء), for I have gained the life imperishable which is not followed by any opposite.' Accordingly, he bids farewell to patience and to the mortal life, because he has quitted the sensible world.

VI

1. When they departed, endurance and patience departed. They departed, although they were dwelling in the core of my heart.
2. I asked them where the travellers rested at noon, and I was answered, 'Their noonday resting-place is where the *shîḥ* and the *bán* trees diffuse a sweet scent.'
3. Then I said to the wind, 'Go and overtake them, for they are biding in the shade of the grove,
4. And bear to them a greeting from a sorrowful man in whose heart are sorrows because he is separated from his people.'

Commentary

1. 'They departed,' i.e. the Divine Ideas (المناظر الالهيّة).

'They were dwelling in the core of my heart': the Divine Ideas have no relationship except with their object (المنظور اليه), which is God; and God dwells in the heart, according to the Tradition 'Neither My earth nor My heaven contains Me, but I am contained in the heart of My servant who believes'. Since, however, no manifestation was vouchsafed to him at this moment, the Ideas, being objects of vision, disappeared, notwithstanding that God was in his heart.

2. 'I asked them,' i.e. the gnostics and the real existences (حقايق) of the past Shaykhs who were my guides on the mystic Way.

'Their noonday resting-place,' etc., i.e. they reposed in every heart where the sighs (انفاس) of longing appeared, for *shîḥ* denotes inclination (*mayl*) and *bán* absence (*bu'd*).

3. 'I said to the wind,' i.e. I sent a sigh of longing after them in the hope of causing them to return to me.

'In the shade of the grove,' i.e. amongst the *arák* trees, whereof the wood is used as a tooth-stick (سواك). He refers to the Tradition 'The use of the tooth-stick purifies the mouth and pleases the Lord', i.e. the Divine Ideas are dwelling in the abode of purity.

VII

1. As I kissed the Black Stone, friendly women thronged around me; they came to perform the circumambulation with veiled faces.
2. They uncovered the (faces like) sunbeams and said to me, 'Beware! for the death of the soul is in thy looking at us.
3. How many aspiring souls have we killed already at al-Muḥaṣṣab of Miná, beside the pebble-heaps,
4. And in Sarḥat al-Wádí and the mountains of Ráma and Jam' and at the dispersion from 'Arafát!
5. Dost not thou see that beauty robs him who hath modesty, and therefore it is called the robber of virtues?
6. Our trysting-place after the circumambulation is at Zamzam beside the midmost tent, beside the rocks.
7. There everyone whom anguish hath emaciated is restored to health by the love-desire that perfumed women stir in him.
8. When they are afraid they let fall their hair, so that they are hidden by their tresses as it were by robes of darkness.'

COMMENTARY

1. 'As I kissed the Black Stone,' i.e. when the Holy Hand (اليمين المقدّسة) was outstretched to me that I might take upon it the Divine oath of allegiance, referring to the verse '*Those who swear fealty to thee swear fealty to God; the hand of God is over their hands*' (Kor. xlviii, 10).

'Friendly women,' i.e. the angels who go round the throne of God (Kor. xxxix, 75).

2. 'The death of the soul,' etc.: these spirits say, 'Do not look at us, lest thou fall passionately in love with us. Thou wert created for God, not for us, and if thou wilt be veiled by us from Him, He will cause thee to pass away from thy existence through Him (افناك عن وجودك به), and thou wilt perish.'

3. 'Have we killed,' i.e. spirits like unto us, for the

above-mentioned angels who go round the Throne have no relationship except with pilgrims circumambulating the Ka'ba.

5. 'Beauty robs him who hath modesty,' since the vision of Beauty enraptures whosoever beholds it.

'The robber of virtues,' i.e. it takes away all delight in the vision of beauty from him who acts at the bidding of the possessor of this beauty; and sometimes the beauteous one bids thee do that which stands between thee and glorious things, inasmuch as those things are gained by means of hateful actions: the Tradition declares that Paradise is encompassed by things which thou dislikest (مَكَارِه).

6. 'At Zamzam,' i.e. in the station of the life which thou yearnest for.

'Beside the midmost tent,' i.e. the intermediate world (البَرْزَخ), which divides the spiritual from the corporeal world.

'Beside the rocks,' i.e. the sensible bodies in which the holy spiritual beings (المعانى القدسيّة) take their abode. He means that these spirits in these imaginary forms are metaphorical and transient, for they vanish from the dreamer as soon as he wakes and from the seer as soon as he returns to his senses. He warns thee not to be deceived by the manifestations of phenomenal beauty, inasmuch as all save God is unreal, i.e. not-being like unto thyself; therefore be His that He may be thine.

7. In the intermediate world (البَرْزَخ) whosoever loves these spiritual beings dwelling in sensible bodies derives refreshment from the world of breaths and scents (عالم الأنفاس والروائح) because the spirit and the form are there united, so that the delight is double.

8. When these phantoms are afraid that their absoluteness will be limited by their confinement in forms, they cause thee to perceive that they are a veil which hides something more subtle than what thou seest, and conceal themselves from thee and quit these forms and once more enjoy infinite freedom.

VIII

1. Their abodes have become decayed, but desire of them is ever new in my heart and decayeth not.
2. These tears are shed over their ruined dwellings, but souls are ever melted at the memory of them.
3. Through love of them I called out behind their riding-camels, 'O ye who are rich in beauty, here am I, a beggar!
4. I have rolled my cheek in the dust in tender and passionate affection: then, by the true love which I owe to you, do not make hopeless
5. One who is drowned in his tears and burned in the fire of sorrow with no respite!'
6. O thou who wouldst kindle a fire, be not hasty! Here is the fire of passion. Go and take of it!

Commentary

1. 'Their abodes have become decayed': he says, 'the places of austerities and mortifications, where the Divine Names made works (اعمال) their abode, have become decayed through age and loss of youthful strength.' The word رُبُوع is used in reference to the springtide (رَبِيع) of human life.

3. 'Behind their riding-camels,' i.e. the powers of youth and the delights of the commencement (البداية).

4. 'I have rolled my cheek in the dust,' i.e. desiring to be united with you, for God says, 'Seek access to Me by means of that which I have not,' viz. abasement and indigence.

6. 'Here is the fire of passion,' i.e. in my heart.

IX

1. Flashes of lightning gleamed to us at al-Abraqán, and their peals of thunder crashed between the ribs.
2. Their clouds poured rain on every meadow and on every quivering branch that bends towards thee.
3. The watercourses were flooded and the breeze wafted

perfume, and a ringdove flapped her wings and a twig put forth leaves.

4. They pitched the red tents between rivulets (creeping) like serpents, amongst which were seated

5. Friendly damsels, bright of countenance, rising like the suns, large-eyed, noble, of generous race, and limber.

COMMENTARY

1. 'Al-Abraqán,' i.e. two manifestations of the Essence, one in the unseen and one in the visible world.

'Flashes of lightning,' referring to the variety of forms in the latter manifestation.

'Peals of thunder,' i.e. the Divine converse (مناجات) which followed the manifestation. This is a Mosaic ecstasy (حالة موسوية), for Moses first saw the fire and afterwards heard God speak. The mention of thunder also signifies that God's speech was a rebuke.

2. 'Their clouds,' i.e. the ecstasies (احوال) which bring forth the Divine sciences.

'On every meadow,' i.e. the heart of man together with the Divine sciences which it holds.

'On every quivering branch,' i.e. the straight movement (الحركة المستقيمة) which is the growth of man (نشأة الانسان), as God says that He created Adam after His own image; and from this station it 'bends', i.e. inclines towards thee that it may instruct thee.

3. He says, 'The valleys of the Divine sciences were flooded, and the world of breaths (عالم الانفاس) diffused the sweet scents of the Divine sciences.'

'A ringdove,' i.e. the Universal Soul together with the effect it produces upon the Partial Soul, which appears in the form of the Universal in so far as it possesses the two faculties of knowledge and action.

'A twig,' i.e. that with which the branches are clothed. He refers to the verse '*Take your becoming vesture at every mosque*' (Kor. vii, 29), i.e. the everlasting vesture of God, which consists in the various kinds of Divine science and gnosis.

4. 'The red tents,' i.e. the bride-like forms of Divine wisdom.

'Rivulets,' i.e. diverse sciences connected with the works which lead to union with these forms of Divine wisdom.

'Like serpents': cf. Kor. xxiv, 44, '*And amongst them is one who walks on his belly.*' He refers to those devout persons who scrupulously examine their food, for by means of pure food which produces strength for the practice of devotion the heart is illuminated and becomes the abode of these forms of Divine wisdom.

5. 'Bright of countenance,' etc., i.e. there is no doubt concerning them, as the Prophet said, 'Ye shall see your Lord as ye see the sun at noonday when no cloud comes between.'

'Noble,' i.e. proceeding from the results of works prescribed by God, unlike the maxims of the philosophers which spring from their own minds.

'Of generous race': عَقِيلة is derived from عَقْل. He means, therefore, that they understand what is imparted to them and perceive its value.

'Limber': although *per se* they are in the station of equilibrium and inflexibility, yet when they are invoked with longing and humility and love they incline towards the caller, because he is not able to ascend to them.

X

1. She said, 'I wonder at a lover who in conceit of his merits
   walks proudly among flowers in a garden.'
2. I replied, 'Do not wonder at what thou seest, for thou
   hast beheld thyself in the mirror of a man.'

Commentary

1. 'Flowers,' i.e. created things.

'A garden,' the unitive station (المقام الجامع), i.e. his essence.

'Utba al-Ghulám used to walk proudly and swagger in his gait. 'How should not I do so,' he said to one who found fault with him, 'since He has become my Lord and I have become His slave?' When a man realizes God in the sense of 'I am His hearing and His sight', this station justifies the attribution to him of whatever is attributed to God.

2. He says, 'I am like a mirror to thee, and in those qualities with which I am invested thou beholdest thyself, not me, but thou beholdest them in my human nature which has received this investiture.'

This is the vision of God in created things, which in the opinion of some is more exalted than the vision of created things in God.

XI

1. O doves that haunt the *arák* and *bán* trees, have pity! Do not double my woes by your lamentation!
2. Have pity! Do not reveal, by wailing and weeping, my hidden desires and my secret sorrows!
3. I respond to her, at eve and morn, with the plaintive cry of a longing man and the moan of an impassioned lover.
4. The spirits faced one another in the thicket of *ghaḍá* trees and bent their branches towards me, and it (the bending) annihilated me;
5. And they brought me divers sorts of tormenting desire and passion and untried affliction.
6. Who will give me sure promise of Jam' and al-Muḥaṣṣab of Miná? Who of Dhát al-Athl? Who of Na'mán?
7. They encompass my heart moment after moment, for the sake of love and anguish, and kiss my pillars,
8. Even as the best of mankind encompassed the Ka'ba, which the evidence of Reason proclaims to be imperfect,
9. And kissed stones therein, although he was a Náṭiq (prophet).[1] And what is the rank of the Temple in comparison with the dignity of Man?

[1] In the Ismá'ílí system Muḥammad, regarded as an incarnation of Universal Reason, is the Náṭiq of the sixth prophetic cycle. See Professor Browne's *Literary History of Persia*, i, 408 seq.

10. How often did they vow and swear that they would not change, but one dyed with henna does not keep oaths.
11. And one of the most wonderful things is a veiled gazelle, who points with red finger-tip and winks with eyelids,
12. A gazelle whose pasture is between the breast-bones and the bowels. O marvel! a garden amidst fires!
13. My heart has become capable of every form: it is a pasture for gazelles and a convent for Christian monks,
14. And a temple for idols and the pilgrim's Ka'ba and the tables of the Tora and the book of the Koran.
15. I follow the religion of Love: whatever way Love's camels take, that is my religion and my faith.
16. We have a pattern in Bishr, the lover of Hind and her sister, and in Qays and Lubná and in Mayya and Ghaylán.

Commentary

1. 'O doves,' i.e. the influences of holiness and purity.

3. 'I respond to her,' i.e. I repeat to her what she says to me, as God said to the soul when He created her, 'Who am I?' and she answered, 'Who am I?' referring to her qualities, whereupon He caused her to dwell four thousand years in the sea of despair and indigence and abasement until she said to Him, 'Thou art my Lord.'

4. 'Faced one another,' because love entails the union of two opposites.

'In the thicket of *ghaḍá* trees,' i.e. the fires of love.

'Branches,' i.e. flames.

'Annihilated me,' in order that He alone might exist, not I, through jealousy that the lover should have any existence in himself apart from his beloved.

6. 'Jam',' i.e. union with the loved ones in the station of proximity, which is al-Muzdalifa.

'Al-Muḥaṣṣab,' the place where the thoughts which prevent lovers from attaining their object of desire are cast out.

'Dhát al-Athl,' referring to the principle (اصل), for it is

the principle in love that thou shouldst be the very essence of thy Beloved and shouldst disappear in Him from thyself.

'Na'mán,' the place of Divine and holy bliss (نعيم).

7. 'For the sake of love and anguish,' i.e. in order to inspire me with passion.

'And kiss my pillars' (properly, kiss over the *lithám* or veil covering the mouth), i.e. he is veiled and unable to behold them except through a medium (واسطة). The 'pillars' are the four elements on which the human constitution is based.[1]

10. 'One dyed with henna': he refers to sensual influences (واردات نفسيّة), such as descended on the soul when God addressed it and said, '*Am not I your Lord?*' (Kor. vii, 171), and received from it a promise and covenant. Then it did not faithfully keep the station of unification (التوحيد), but followed other gods. No one was exempt from this polytheism, for every one said, 'I did' and 'I said', at the time when he forgot to contemplate the Divine Agent and Speaker within him.

11. 'A veiled gazelle,' i.e. a Divine subtlety (لطيفة) veiled by a sensual state (حالة نفسيّة), in reference to the unknown spiritual feelings (احوال) of gnostics, who cannot explain their feelings to other men; they can only indicate them symbolically to those who have begun to experience the like.

'With red finger-tip': he means the same thing as he meant by 'one dyed with henna' in the last verse.

'And winks with eyelids,' i.e. the speculative proofs concerning the principles of gnostics are valid only for those who have already been imbued with the rudiments of this experience. Gnostics, though they resemble the vulgar outwardly, are Divines (ربّانيّون) inwardly.

12. 'Whose pasture,' etc., as 'Alí said, striking his breast, 'Here are sciences in plenty, could I but find people to carry them (in their minds).'

[1] The author leaves the next two verses unexplained. 'The best of mankind' is Muḥammad.

'A garden amidst fires,' i.e. manifold sciences which, strange to say, are not consumed by the flames of love in his breast. The reason is, that these sciences are produced by the fires of seeking and longing, and therefore, like the salamander, are not destroyed by them.

13. 'My heart has become capable of every form,' as another has said, 'The heart (القلب) is so called from its changing (تقلّبه),' for it varies according to the various influences by which it is affected in consequence of the variety of its states of feeling (احوال); and the variety of its feelings is due to the variety of the Divine manifestations that appear to its inmost ground (سِرّ). The religious law gives to this phenomenon the name of 'transformation' (التحوّل والتبدّل فى الصور).

'A pasture for gazelles,' i.e. for the objects of his love.

'A convent for Christian monks': inasmuch as he makes the loved ones to be monks, he calls the heart a convent.

14. 'A temple for idols,' i.e. for the Divine Realities which men seek and for whose sake they worship God.

'The pilgrim's Ka'ba,' because his heart is encompassed by exalted spirits.

'The tables of the Tora,' i.e. his heart is a table on which are inscribed the Mosaic sciences that have accrued to him.

'The book of the Koran,' because his heart has received an inheritance of the perfect Muḥammadan knowledge.

15. 'I follow the religion of Love,' in reference to the verse '*Follow me, then God will love you*' (Kor. iii, 29).

'Whatever way Love's camels take,' etc., i.e. 'I accept willingly and gladly whatever burden He lays upon me. No religion is more sublime than a religion based on love and longing for Him whom I worship and in whom I have faith'. This is a peculiar prerogative of Moslems, for the station of perfect love is appropriated to Muḥammad beyond any other prophet, since God took him as His beloved (حبيبًا).

16. He says, 'Love, *quâ* love, is one and the same reality to those Arab lovers and to me, but the objects of our love

are different, for they loved a phenomenon, whereas I love the Essential.' 'We have a pattern in them,' because God only afflicted them with love for human beings like themselves in order that He might show, by means of them, the falseness of those who pretend to love Him and yet feel no such transport and rapture in loving Him as deprived those enamoured men of their reason and made them unconscious of themselves.

XII

1. At Dhú Salam and the monastery in the abode of al-Ḥimá are gazelles who show thee the sun in the forms of marble statues.
2. Therefore I watch spheres and serve in a church and guard a many-coloured meadow in the spring.
3. And at one time I am called the herdsman of the gazelles in the desert, and at another time I am called a Christian monk and an astrologer.
4. My Beloved is three although He is One, even as the (three) Persons (of the Trinity) are made one Person in essence.
5. So be not displeased, O friend, that I speak of gazelles, that move round the marble statues as 'a shining sun',
6. Or that I use metaphorically the necks of the gazelles, the face of the sun, and the breast and wrist of the white statue,
7. Just as I have lent to the branches (spiritual) endowments and to the meadows moral qualities, and to the lightning laughing lips.

Commentary

1. 'Dhú Salam': a station to which submission is rendered on account of its beauty.

'The monastery,' referring to a Syrian ecstasy (حالة سريانيّة).

'The abode of al-Ḥimá,' that which surrounds the most inaccessible veil of Divine glory.

'Gazelles,' i.e. forms of Divine and prophetic wisdom which descend upon his spirit.

'Marble statues,' i.e. sorts of knowledge (معارف) with which neither reason nor lust is connected; hence he makes them inanimate (جمادية).

2. 'I watch spheres,' i.e. the spiritual states in which these sorts of knowledge revolve, like the sun.

'And serve in a church,' because marble effigies are found in churches.

'And guard,' etc.: the meadows where these gazelles pasture are the scenes of devotional acts and Divine morals; they are described as 'many-coloured', i.e. adorned with the Divine realities, and spring-like, because that which is new and fresh is more delightful to the soul.

3. He refers to his ever-changing spiritual states, which bring with them manifold Divine influences and sciences. Although the spiritual experiences vary, the Divine substance (العين) remains one. This is the 'transformation' (التحوّل فى الصور) of which Muslim speaks in the chapter on Faith, Those who worship God in the sun behold a sun, and those who worship Him in living things see a living thing, and those who worship Him in inanimate objects see an inanimate object, and those who worship Him as a Being unique and unparalleled see that which has no like.

4. He says, 'Number does not beget multiplicity in the Divine substance, as the Christians declare that the Three Persons of the Trinity are One God, and as the Koran declares (xvii, 110): "*Call on God or call on the Merciful; howsoever ye invoke Him, it is well, for to Him belong the most excellent Names.*"' The cardinal Names in the Koran are three, viz. Allah and ar-Raḥmán and ar-Rabb, by which One God is signified, and the rest of the Names serve as epithets of those three.

6. 'Necks,' indicating the Light (النور), as in the Tradition 'The muezzins shall be the longest-necked of mankind on the Day of Resurrection'.

'The face of the sun,' as in the Tradition 'Ye shall see your Lord as ye see the sun'.

'The breast and wrist of the white statue,' as in the Tradition which mentions the breast and fore-arm of the Almighty.

7. 'The branches,' i.e. the souls distraught by the majesty of God and turned away by love from the consciousness of their personality and from the contemplation of their phenomenal nature.

'The meadow,' i.e. the station of union (مقام الجمع) in which God has placed them.

'Moral qualities,' i.e. the scented breaths of Divine Mercy, viz. the goodly praise (الثناء الجميل) of the kind mentioned in the Tradition 'Even as Thou dost praise Thyself'.

'The lightning,' i.e. a manifestation of the Divine Essence.

'Laughing lips,' as God is said in the Tradition to rejoice at the repentance of His servant, or to laugh (الله يضحك).

XIII

1. A ringdove wailed and a sad lover complained, and he was grieved by her trilling note and complaint.
2. Tears flowed from their eyes in distress for her complaint, and 'twas as tho' they (the tears) were fountains.
3. I responded to her in the bereavement caused by the loss of her only child: one who loses an only child is bereaved indeed.
4. I responded to her, while Grief walked between us; she was invisible, but I was clearly seen.
5. In me is a burning desire, from love of the sandy tract of 'Álij, where her tents are and the large-eyed maidens,
6. With murderous glances, languishing: their eyelids are sheaths for glances like swords.
7. I did not cease to swallow the tears proceeding from my malady and to conceal and guard my passion from those who blame me,
8. Until, when the raven's croak announced their departure, separation exposed the desire of a sorrow-stricken lover.

9. They journeyed continuously through the night, they cut the nose-rings of their camels, so that they (the camels) moaned and cried under the litters.
10. I beheld the pangs of death at the time when they loosed the camels' reins and tied their saddle-girths.
11. Oh! separation together with love's pain is mortal, but love's sorest pain together with meeting is light.
12. None blames me for desiring her, for she is beloved and beautiful wherever she may be.

Commentary

1. 'A ringdove,' i.e. the Universal Spirit, born of God and breathed into Man. She is described as having a collar (ring), in reference to the covenant which He laid upon her.

'A sad lover,' i.e. the partial spirit which is in Man.

'Her trilling note,' i.e. the sweet melodies calling him to union with her. This union is the first resurrection at death (الحشر الاوّل بالموت).

2. 'From their eyes': he refers to the partial spirits (الارواح الجزئيّة). 'Her complaint': the Universal Spirit, which is the father of the partial spirits, longs for them even more than they long for her.

3. 'Her only child,' i.e. the special quality which distinguishes her from all things else, viz. her unity (وحدانيّة), whereby she knows the unity of Him who brought her into being. The loss of it consists in her not knowing what it is and in its not being plainly discerned by her.

4. 'She was invisible,' for she does not belong to the world of expression and exposition.

5. 'The sandy tract of 'Álij,' i.e. the subtleties of the acquired or analytic sciences. 'Álij refers to the striving after good works (معالجة الاعمال).

'Her tents,' the veils which conceal these sciences.

'The large-eyed maidens,' i.e. the sciences which descend upon the solitary recluse.

6. 'With murderous glances,' i.e. they cause him to pass away from his own personality.

'Languishing,' i.e. they incline towards the solitary. The term 'glances' indicates that they are sciences of contemplation and revelation, not of faith and mystery, and that they proceed from the manifestation of forms.

7. He refers to a state of concealment which is characteristic of the Malámatís.[1]

9. 'They journeyed continuously': since the object sought is infinite, the return from it is also a journey towards it. There is no migration except from one Divine Name to another.

'They cut the nose-rings of their camels,' on account of the violent haste with which they travelled.

11. 'Meeting,' a kind of presence (حضور) in which there is no passing away (فناء).

12. He says, 'The aspirations and desires of all seekers are attached to Her, yet She is essentially unknown to them hence they all love Her, yet none blames another for loving Her. Similarly, every individual soul and the adherents of every religion seek salvation, but since they do not know it they are also ignorant of the way that leads to it, though everyone believes that he is on the right way. All strife between people of different religions and sects is about the way that leads to salvation, not about salvation itself. If anyone knew that he was taking the wrong way, he would not persevere in his error.' Accordingly the author says that She manifests Herself everywhere, like the sun, and that every person who beholds Her deems that She is with him in Her essence, so that envy and jealousy are removed from their hearts.

XIV

1. He saw the lightning in the east and he longed for the east, but if it had flashed in the west he would have longed for the west.

[1] A Ṣúfí sect or school who emphasized the need of incurring blame (*malámat*) for God's sake and of concealing spiritual merit, lest they should fall into self-conceit. See my translation of the *Kashf al-Maḥjúb*, pp. 62-9.

2. My desire is for the lightning and its gleam, not for the places and the earth.
3. The east wind related to me from them a tradition handed down successively from distracted thoughts, from my passion, from anguish, from my tribulation,
4. From rapture, from my reason, from yearning, from ardour, from tears, from my eyelid, from fire, from my heart,
5. That 'He whom thou lovest is between thy ribs; the breaths toss him from side to side'.
6. I said to the east wind, 'Bring a message to him and say that he is the enkindler of the fire within my heart.
7. If it shall be quenched, then everlasting union, and if it shall burn, then no blame to the lover!'

Commentary

1. He refers to the vision of God in created things, viz. the manifestation in forms, and this causes him to cleave to phenomena, because the manifestation appears in them.

'The east,' i.e. the place of phenomenal manifestation.

'If it had flashed in the west,' i.e. if it had been a manifestation of the Divine essence to the lover's heart, he would have longed for that purer manifestation in the world of purity and mystery.

2. He says, 'I desire the forms in which the manifestation takes place only in so far as they are a *locus* for the manifestation itself.'

3. The world of breaths (عالم الانفاس) communicated to me the inward meaning of these phenomenal forms.

4. 'Rapture' (literally, 'intoxication,' سُكر): the fourth degree in the manifestations. The first degree is ذوق, the second شُرب, and the third ری.

'From my reason,' because intoxication transports the reason and takes away from it whatever it has.

5. 'The breaths,' etc., i.e. the overwhelming awe inspired by this manifestation produces in him various ecstasies (احوال).

7. He says, 'If the awful might of this manifestation shall be veiled through the permanence of the Divine

substance, then the union will be lasting; but if the manifestation be unchecked, it will sweep away all that exists in its *locus*, and those who perish are not in fault.' This is the saying of one possessed and mastered by ecstasy.

XV

1. They left me at al-Uthayl and al-Naqá shedding tears and complaining of the fire (that consumed me).
2. My father be the ransom of him for whose sake I melted with anguish! My father be the ransom of him for whose sake I died of fear!
3. The blush of shame on his cheek is the whiteness of dawn conversing with the redness of eve.
4. Patience decamped and grief pitched tents, and I lie prostrate between these two.
5. Who will compose my distracted thoughts? Who will relieve my pain? Guide me to him! Who will ease my sorrow? Who will help a passionate lover?
6. Whenever I keep secret the torments of desire, my tears betray the flame within and the sleeplessness.
7. And whenever I say, 'Give me one look!' the answer is, 'Thou art not hindered but for pity's sake.'
8. It cannot be that one look from them will avail thee. Is it aught but the glimpse of a levin that flashed?
9. I am not forgetting the time when the camel-driver, wishing for separation and seeking al-Abraq, urged them on.
10. The ravens of separation croaked at them—may God not preserve a raven that croaked!
11. The raven of separation is only a camel which carried away the loved ones with a swift wide-stepping pace.

Commentary

1. He laments the departure of his companions, viz. the spiritual angelic beings who suffer no natural bondage, whilst he is left a prisoner in this body, occupied with governing it and prevented from wandering freely through the celestial spheres.

'Al-Uthayl,' his natural constitution (اصله الطبيعى).

'Al-Naqá,' his body.

2. 'My father,' i.e. the Highest Spirit (الروح الاعلى), which is his real father in the world above and his phenomenal mother in the world below.

'Of him for whose sake I melted with anguish': he refers to the Divine mystery contained in his heart.

'Of fear,' i.e. fear of the radiance of the Divine majesty.

6. The love that is revealed is stronger and more passionate, for there is no good in a love that is ruled by reason.

7. God in His mercy veils the splendours of His face from His creatures.

8. The more the Beloved looks on thee, the more is thy anguish increased. Vision is possible only in moments of ecstasy.

9. 'The camel-driver,' i.e. the voice of God calling those exalted spiritual beings to ascend towards Him.

'Separation,' i.e. their departure from the phenomenal world.

'Al-Abraq,' the place where God is manifested in His essence.

10. 'The ravens of separation,' i.e. considerations affecting his phenomenal existence, which hinder him from the ascent to God.

11. 'A camel,' i.e. the ravens of separation are really a man's aspirations (هِمَم), since aspiration bears him aloft and unites him with the object of his search.

XVI

1. They (the women) mounted the howdahs on the swift camels and placed in them the (damsels like) marble statues and full moons,
2. And promised my heart that they should return; but do the fair promise anything except deceit?
3. And she saluted with her henna-tipped fingers for the leave-taking, and let fall tears that excited the flames (of desire).

4. When she turned her back with the purpose of making for al-Khawarnaq and as-Sadír,
5. I cried out after them, 'Perdition!' She answered and said, 'Dost thou invoke perdition?
6. Then invoke it not only once, but cry "Perdition!" many times.'
7. O dove of the *arák* trees, have a little pity on me! for parting only increased thy moans,
8. And thy lamentation, O dove, inflames the longing lover, excites the jealous,
9. Melts the heart, drives off sleep, and doubles our desires and sighing.
10. Death hovers because of the dove's lamentation, and we beg him to spare us a little while,
11. That perchance a breath from the zephyr of Ḥájir may sweep towards us rain-clouds,
12. By means of which thou wilt satisfy thirsty souls; but thy clouds only flee farther than before.
13. O watcher of the star, be my boon-companion, and O wakeful spy on the lightning, be my nocturnal comrade!
14. O sleeper in the night, thou didst welcome sleep and inhabit the tombs ere thy death.
15. But hadst thou been in love with the fond maiden, thou wouldst have gained, through her, happiness and joy,
16. Giving to the fair (women) the wines of intimacy, conversing secretly with the suns, and flattering the full moons.

COMMENTARY

1. 'The camels' are the human faculties, 'the howdahs' are the actions which they are charged to perform, 'the damsels' in the howdahs are the mystical sciences and the perfect sorts of knowledge.

3. He says, 'This Divine subtlety, being acquired and not given directly, is subject to a change produced by contact with phenomena'; this change he indicates by speaking of 'her henna-tipped fingers', as though it were the modification

of unity by a kind of association (اشتراک). Nevertheless, her staying in the heart is more desirable than her going, for she protects the gnostic as long as she is there.

'And let fall tears,' etc.: she let loose in the heart sciences of contemplation which produced an intense yearning.

4. 'Al-Khawarnaq and as-Sadír,' i.e. the Divine presence.

5. 'Perdition!' i.e. death to the phenomenal world now that these sublime mysteries have vanished from it.

'Dost thou invoke perdition?' i.e. why dost thou not see the face of God in everything, in light and darkness, in simple and composite, in subtle and gross, in order that thou mayst not feel the grief of parting.

6. 'Cry "Perdition!" many times' (cf. Kor. xxv, 15), i.e. not only in this station but in every station in which thou art placed, for thou must bid farewell to every one of them, and thou canst not fail to be grieved, since, whenever the form of the Truth disappears from thee, thou imaginest that He has left thee; but He has not left thee, and it is only thy remaining with thyself (بقونک معک) that veils from thee the vision of that which pervades the whole of creation.

7. 'O dove of the *arák* trees': he addresses holy influences of Divine pleasure which have descended upon him.

'Have a little pity on me!' i.e. pity my weakness and inability to attain unto thy purity.

'For parting only increased thy moans': he says, 'Inasmuch as thy substance only exists through and in me, and I am diverted from thee by the dark world of phenomena which keeps me in bondage, for this cause thou art lamenting thy separation from me.'

8. 'And thy lamentation,' etc., i.e. we who seek the unbounded freedom of the celestial world should weep more bitterly than thou.

'Excites the jealous': jealousy arises from regarding others (الاغيار), and he who beholds God in everything feels no jealousy, for God is One; but since God manifests Himself in various forms, the term 'jealousy' is applicable to Him.

10. 'Death,' i.e. the station in which the subtle principle of Man is severed from its governance of this dark body for the sake of the Divine subtleties which are conveyed to it by the above-mentioned holy influences.

11. 'Ḥájir' denotes here the most inaccessible veil of the Divine glory. No phenomenal being can attain to the immediate experience thereof, but scents of it blow over the hearts of gnostics in virtue of a kind of amorous affection (بضرب من التعشّق).

'Rain-clouds,' i.e. sciences and diverse sorts of knowledge belonging to the most holy Essence.

13. 'O watcher of the star,' in reference to keeping in mind that which the sciences offer in their various connexions.

'O wakeful spy on the lightning': the lightning is a *locus* of manifestation of the Essence. The author says, addressing one who seeks it, 'Our quest is the same, be my comrade in the night.'

14. This verse may be applied either to the heedless (اهل الغفلة) or to the unconscious (اهل الفناء).

15. 'The fond maiden,' i.e. the Essential subtlety which is the gnostic's object of desire.

'Through her': although She is unattainable, yet through her manifestation to thee all that thou hast is baptized for thee (ينصبغ لك), and thy whole kingdom is displayed to thee by that Essential form.

16. 'Conversing secretly with the suns,' etc., in reference to the Traditions which declare that God will be seen in the next world like the sun in a cloudless sky or like the moon when she is full.

XVII

1. O driver of the reddish-white camels, do not hasten with them, but stop! for I am a cripple going after them.
2. Stop the camels and tighten their reins! I beseech thee by God, by my passion, by my anguish, O driver!
3. My soul is willing, but my foot does not second her. Who will pity and help me?

4. What shall the skilled craftsman do in a case where his tools have declared themselves to be working mischief?
5. Turn aside, for their tents are on the right of the valley. God bless thee, O valley, for what thou containest!
6. Thou hast collected a folk who are my soul and my breath and the inmost core of the black clot in the membrane of my liver.
7. May my love be unblest if I do not die of grief at Ḥájir or Salʿ or Ajyád!

Commentary

1. The Divine Spirit which speaks in Man and is charged with the governance of this body says to the camel-driver, i.e. to God's summoner who guides the lofty aspirations in their journey heavenward, 'Do not hasten with them, for I am hampered by this body to which I am tied until death.'

3. 'Who will pity and help me?' He refers to the decree of God (القدر).

4. He says, 'What shall I do? Though I am able to quit the body at times, i.e. in moments of passing away and absence (الفنآء, الغيبة) under the influence of ecstasy, my aim is to depart entirely; and, moreover, at such moments the sensible world exercises a powerful attraction upon me. This attraction (here called "his tools") spoils what I am endeavouring to do, and disturbs my state of passing away and absence in order to bring me back to the body.'

5. 'Their tents,' i.e. the abodes of these aspirations, which are in their knowledge of God, not in God, since He is not a *locus* for anything. Knowledge of God is the utmost goal to which contingent being can attain, and the whole universe depends on knowledge and on nothing else.

'On the right of the valley,' referring to the occasion when God spoke to Moses at Mount Sinai (Kor. xix, 53).

'What thou containest,' i.e. Divine, holy, and Mosaic kinds of knowledge.

7. 'Ḥájir,' i.e. the intermediate world (البرزخ).

'Sal',' a mountain near Medina, i.e. the station of Muḥammad.

'Ajyád,' a mountain near Mecca, i.e. a Divine station which causes me to pass away from all phenomenal existence.

XVIII

1. Halt at the abodes and weep over the ruins and ask the decayed habitations a question.
2. 'Where are the loved ones? Where are their camels gone?' (They answer), 'Behold them traversing the vapour in the desert.
3. Thou seest them in the mirage like gardens: the vapour makes large in the eyes the figure (of one who walks in it).'
4. They went, desiring al-'Udhayb, that they might drink there a cool life-giving fountain.
5. I followed, asking the zephyr about them, whether they have pitched tents or have sought the shade of the *ḍál* tree.
6. The zephyr said, 'I left their tents at Zarúd, and the camels were complaining of fatigue from their night-journey.
7. They had let down over the tents coverings to protect their beauty from the heat of noon.
8. Rise, then, and go towards them, seeking their traces, and drive thy camels speedily in their direction.
9. And when thou wilt stop at the landmarks of Ḥájir and cross dales and hills there,
10. Their abodes will be near and their fire will be clearly seen—a fire which has caused the flame of love to blaze.
11. Make the camels kneel! Let not its lions affright thee, for longing love will present them to thine eyes in the form of cubs.'

Commentary

1. He says to the voice of God (داعي الحقّ) calling from his heart, 'Halt at the abodes,' i.e. the stations where gnostics

alight in the course of their journey to infinite knowledge of their object of worship.

'And weep over the ruins,' i.e. the traces left by those gnostics, since I cannot accompany them.

'The decayed habitations,' because there is no joy in the abodes which have been deserted, and their very existence depends on those who dwell in them.

2. 'Their camels,' i.e. their aspirations.

'The vapour,' i.e. the evidences (دلائل) of that which they seek, for its evidences are attached to its being found in themselves.

'The desert,' i.e. the station of abstraction (تجريد).

3. 'Makes large,' i.e. they are grand because they give evidence of the grandeur of that which they seek. Hence it is said, 'In order that he who was not (namely, thou) may pass away, and He who never was not (namely, God) may subsist for ever.' And God said, '*Like a vapour in the plain* (i.e. the station of humility) . . . *when he cometh to it, he findeth it to be nothing, but he findeth God with him*' (Kor. xxiv, 39), inasmuch as all secondary causes have been cut off from him. Accordingly the author says that the vapour makes large, etc., meaning that Man's superiority over all other contingent beings consists in his giving stronger evidence of God, since he is the most perfect organism, as the Prophet said, 'Verily he was created in the image of the Merciful.'

4. 'Desiring al-'Udhayb,' i.e. seeking the mystery of life in the station of purity from the fountain of liberality.

'That they might drink': *shurb* is the second degree of Divine manifestation (التجلّى), *dhawq* being the first.

5. 'Whether they have pitched tents,' referring to knowledge acquired by them.

'Or have sought the shade of the *ḍál* tree,' referring to knowledge divinely bestowed, in which their actions have no part. *Ḍál* implies bewilderment (حيرة).

6. 'At Zarúd,' a great tract of sand in the desert: inasmuch as sand is often tossed by the wind from one place

to another, he indicates that they are in a state of unrest, because they are seeking that which is unimaginable, and of which only the traces are to be found in the soul.

7. 'Coverings to protect their beauty,' i.e. unless their faces, viz. their realities, were veiled, the intense radiance of this station would consume them.

8. 'Seeking their traces': he says, 'Seek to approach the degree of the prophets with thy aspiration (this he indicates by the word "camels"), but not by immediate experience (حال), for only the Prophet has immediate experience of this station.' There is nothing, however, to prevent any-one from aspiring to it, although it is unattainable.

9. 'Ḥájir,' referring to the obstacle which makes immediate experience of this station impossible for us.

10. 'Their fire will be clearly seen,' i.e. the perils into which they plunged before they could arrive at these abodes. According to the Tradition, 'Paradise is encompassed with hateful actions.'

One of the illuminati (المكاشَفين) told me at al-Mawṣil that he had seen in a dream Ma'rúf al-Karkhí sitting in the midst of Hell-fire. The dream terrified him and he did not perceive its meaning. I said to him, 'That fire is the enclosure that guards the abode in which you saw him seated. Let any-one who desires to reach that abode plunge into the fire.' My friend was pleased with this explanation and recognized that it was true.

11. 'Let not its lions affright thee,' i.e. if thou art a true lover be not dismayed by the dangers confronting thee. 'In the form of cubs,' i.e. innocuous and of no account.

XIX

1. O mouldering remains (of the encampment) at al-Uthayl,
   where I played with friendly maidens!
2. Yesterday it was cheerful and smiling, but to-day it has
   become desolate and frowning.
3. They went far away and I was unaware of them, and they
   knew not that my mind was watching over them,

4. Following them wherever they journeyed and pitched tents, and sometimes it was managing the beasts of burden,
5. Until, when they alighted in a barren wilderness and pitched tents and spread the carpets,
6. It brought them back to a meadow verdant and ripe which erstwhile had been an arid desert.
7. They did not halt at any place but its meadow contained forms beautiful as peacocks,
8. And they did not depart from any place but its earth contained tombs of their lovers.

Commentary

1. 'Al-Uthayl,' i.e. the natural constitution. Its remains are described as 'mouldering' because they are changed by the various spiritual emotions (احوال) which pass over them.

'Friendly maidens,' i.e. forms of Divine wisdom by which the gnostic's heart is gladdened.

2. 'Desolate and frowning,' because he has returned to the world of sense and consciousness.

3. 'And they knew not,' etc.: as, when a man leaves a place, he remains there in imagination and keeps the picture of it in his soul.

4. 'It was managing the beasts of burden,' i.e. he was influencing them by his thought, so that their thoughts turned to him. This was the result of his sincerity; for the inferior, if he turn sincerely to God, may influence the superior, as often happens with sincere novices and their spiritual directors.

5. 'In a barren wilderness,' i.e. the station of absolute and abstract unification.

'And spread the carpets,' in reference to the Divine favours which they received on reaching the abode of the Truth.

6. In this verse he points out that no reality except the Divine substance can subsist together with abstract unification. Hence, when they gained this station and realized it and knew the meaning of God's word, '*There is nothing like unto*

Him,' He brought them back to the unification of their own essences in respect of their oneness, which is incomparable in respect of the Divine substance contained in its essence.

'To a meadow verdant and ripe,' referring to the Divine mysteries which the Truth conveyed to them by the realities of the Names.

7. 'Forms beautiful as peacocks,' i.e. their lovely spiritual states, actions, and dispositions.

8. 'Tombs of their lovers,' i.e. the realities which desire that their traces should be manifested in gnostics. These objects of knowledge only exist through those who know them, and therefore they love the existence of the gnostic, in so far as he knows them, more intensely than they are desired by him. Accordingly the author describes them as dying when the gnostics depart.

XX

1. My lovesickness is from her of the lovesick eyelids: console me by the mention of her, console me!
2. The grey doves fluttered in the meadows and wailed: the grief of these doves is from that which grieved me.
3. May my father be the ransom of a tender playful girl, one of the maidens guarded in howdahs, advancing swayingly among the married women!
4. She rose, plain to see, like a sun, and when she vanished she shone in the horizon of my heart.
5. O ruined abodes at Ráma! How many fair damsels with swelling breasts have they beheld!
6. May my father and I myself be the ransom of a God-nurtured gazelle which pastures between my ribs in safety!
7. The fire thereof in that place is light: thus is the light the quencher of the fires.
8. O my two friends, bend my reins aside that I may see the form of her abode with clear vision.
9. And when ye reach the abode, descend, and there, my two companions, weep for me,

10. And stop with me a little while at the ruins, that we may endeavour to weep, nay, that I may weep indeed because of that which befell me.
11. Passion shoots me without arrows, passion slays me without a spear.
12. Tell me, will ye weep with me when I weep beside her? Help me, oh help me to weep!
13. And rehearse to me the tale of Hind and Lubná and Sulaymá and Zaynab and 'Inán!
14. Then tell me further of Ḥájir and Zarúd, give me news of the pastures of the gazelles!
15. And mourn for me with the poetry of Qays and Lubná, and with Mayya and the afflicted Ghaylán!
16. Long have I yearned for a tender maiden, endowed with prose and verse, having a pulpit, eloquent,
17. One of the princesses from the land of Persia, from the most glorious of cities, from Iṣfahán.
18. She is the daughter of 'Iráq, the daughter of my Imám, and I am her opposite, a child of Yemen.
19. O my lords, have ye seen or heard that two opposites are ever united?
20. Had you seen us at Ráma proffering each other cups of passion without fingers,
21. Whilst passion caused sweet and joyous words to be uttered between us without a tongue,
22. You would have seen a state in which the understanding disappears—Yemen and 'Iráq embracing together.
23. Falsely spoke the poet[1] who said before my time (and he has pelted me with the stones of his understanding),
24. 'O thou who givest the Pleiades in marriage to Suhayl, God bless thee! how should they meet?
25. The Pleiades are in the north whenever they rise, and Suhayl whenever he rises is in the south.'

[1] 'Umar b. Abí Rabí'a, ed. by Schwarz, vol. ii, p. 247, No. 439.

COMMENTARY

1. 'Her of the lovesick eyelids': he means the Presence desired by gnostics. Although she is too sublime to be known and loved, she inclines towards them in mercy and kindness and descends into their hearts by a sort of manifestation.

'Console me by the mention of her': there is no cure for his malady but remembrance (ذكر). He says 'Console me' twice, i.e. by my remembrance of God and by God's remembrance of me (cf. Kor. ii, 147).

2. 'The grey doves,' i.e. the spirits of the intermediate world.

'And wailed,' because their souls cannot join the spirits which have been released from imprisonment in this earthly body.

3. 'A tender playful girl,' i.e. a form of Divine wisdom, essential and holy, which fills the heart with joy.

'One of the maidens guarded in howdahs': she is a virgin, because none has ever known her before; she was veiled in modesty and jealousy during all her journey from the Divine Presence to the heart of this gnostic.

'The married women,' i.e. the forms of Divine wisdom already realized by gnostics who preceded him.

4. 'And when she vanished,' etc., i.e. when she set in the world of evidence (عالم الشهادة) she rose in the world of the Unseen (عالم الغيب).

5. 'O ruined abodes,' i.e. the bodily faculties.

'At Ráma,' from رام (he sought), implying that their search is vain.

'How many fair damsels,' etc., i.e. subtle and Divine forms by which the bodily faculties were annihilated.

7. The natural fires are extinguished by the heavenly light in his heart.

8. 'The form of her abode,' i.e. the Presence from which she issued forth. He seems to desire the station of Divine contemplation, since wisdom is not desired except for the sake of that to which it leads.

9. 'Weep for me,' because this Presence annihilates everyone who attains unto her and beholds her.

10. 'That I may weep,' etc., i.e. for the loss of the loved ones and of everything except the ruins of their abode.

11. 'Without arrows,' i.e. from a distance. He refers to the state called شَوْق.

'Without a spear,' i.e. near at hand. He refers to the state called اشتياق.

13. Hind was the mistress of Bishr, and Lubná of Qays b. al-Dharíḥ; 'Inán was a slave-girl belonging to an-Náṭifí; Zaynab was one of the mistresses of 'Umar b. Abí Rabí'a; Sulaymá was a slave-girl whom the author had seen: he says that she had a lover. He interprets the names of all these women mystically, e.g. Hind is explained as an allusion to the Fall of Adam, and Zaynab as signifying removal from the station of saintship to that of prophecy.

16. He describes this essential knowledge (المعرفة الذاتيّة) as endowed with prose and verse, i.e. absolute in respect of her essence, but limited in respect of possession (من حيث الملك).

'A pulpit,' i.e. the ladder of the Most Beautiful Names. To climb this ladder is to be invested with the qualities of these Names.

'Eloquent,' referring to the station of Apostleship.

The author adds: 'I allude enigmatically to the various kinds of mystical knowledge which are under the veil of an-Niẓám, the maiden daughter of our Shaykh.'

17. 'One of the princesses,' on account of her asceticism, for ascetics are the kings of the earth.

18. ''Iráq' indicates origin, i.e. this knowledge comes of a noble race.

'A child of Yemen,' i.e. in respect of faith (ايمان) and wisdom and the breath of the Merciful (نفس الرحمن) and tenderness of heart. These qualities are the opposite of what is attributed to 'Iráq, viz. rudeness and severity and infidelity, whereas the opposite of 'Iráq itself is not Yemen, but the Maghrib, and the opposite of Yemen itself is not 'Iráq, but Syria. The antithesis here is between the qualities of the Beloved and those of the lover.

19. 'Two opposites,' referring to the story of Junayd, when a man sneezed in his presence and said, '*God be praised!*' (Kor. i, 1). Junayd said, completing the verse, '*Who is the Lord of created beings.*' The man replied, 'And who is the created being, that he should be mentioned in the same breath with God?' 'O my brother,' said Junayd, 'the phenomenal, when it is joined to the Eternal, vanishes and leaves no trace behind. When He is there, thou art not, and if thou art there, He is not.'

22. 'Yemen and 'Iráq,' etc., i.e. the identification (اتّحاد) of the qualities of Wrath and Mercy. He refers to the saying of Abú Sa'íd al-Kharráz, who on being asked how he knew God, answered, 'By His uniting two opposites, for *He is the First and the Last and the Outward and the Inward*' (Kor. lvii, 3).

24. 'The Pleiades,' i.e. the seven attributes demonstrated by scholastic philosophers.

'Suhayl,' i.e. the Divine Essence.

25. 'In the north,' i.e. in the world of phenomena. The Divine attributes are manifested in Creation, but the Divine Essence does not enter into Creation.

XXI

1. O garden of the valley, answer the lady of the preserve and her who hath shining front-teeth, O garden of the valley!
2. And let a little of thy shades o'ershadow her for a short time until she be settled in the meeting-place.
3. And her tents be pitched in thy midst. Then thou wilt have as much as thou wishest of dew to feed the tender shoots,
4. And as much as thou wishest of showers and the moisture of clouds passing over her *bán* trees at eve and morn,

5. And as much as thou wishest of dense shade and fruit, delicious to the gatherer, swaying the bough (on which it hangs),
6. And of those who seek Zarúd and its sands, and of those who chant as they drive the camels from behind, and of those who march in front and lead them well.

COMMENTARY

1. 'O garden of the valley,' in reference to the bush in which the Divine light appeared to Moses.

'The lady of the preserve,' i.e. the reality of Moses, signifying a spiritual degree which the gnostic inherited from Moses. 'Preserve' denotes the station of Glory unattainable by his essence.

'Shining front-teeth,' because he is in the station of converse and speech (المناجاة والكلام).

2. 'Until she be settled,' i.e. until the place be ready for her reception, so that she may speak from his essence to his essence without regard to anything extraneous.

3. 'Dew to feed the tender shoots,' i.e. gracious sorts of knowledge which nourish the human organism.

6. 'Zarúd and its sands,' i.e. elusive sorts of knowledge which are not to be apprehended save in moments of ecstasy.

'And of those who chant,' etc. The *hádí* who drives the camels from behind typifies that which comes with fear and chiding and menaces, while the *hádí* who goes in front of the camels typifies that which comes with hope and joy and kindness. The former is the servant of the Wrathful (عبد القهّار), and the latter is the servant of the Merciful (عبد اللطيف).

XXII

1. Turn the camels aside towards the stony tract of Thahmad, where are the tender branches and the humid meadow,
2. Where the lightnings show to thee their flashes, where the clouds pass at eve and morn,
3. And lift thy voice at dawn to invoke the bright-faced damsels and the fair lissome virgins,

4. Who murder with their black eyes and bend their supple necks.
5. Among them is she who loves and assails with glances like arrows and Indian swords every frenzied heart that loves the fair.
6. She takes with a hand soft and delicate, like pure silk, anointed with *nadd* and shredded musk.
7. When she looks, she gazes with the deep eye of a young gazelle; to her eye belongs the blackness of antimony.
8. Her eyes are adorned with languishment and killing magic, her sides are girt with amazement and incomparable beauty.
9. A slender one, she loves not that which I love and she does not fulfil her threats with sincerity.[1]
10. She let down her plaited lock as a black serpent, that she might frighten with it those who were following her.
11. By God, I fear not death; my only fear is that I shall die and shall not see her to-morrow.

Commentary

1. 'The camels,' i.e. the clouds.

2. 'The lightnings.' The author of these poems always uses the term 'lightning' to denote a centre of manifestation for the Divine Essence.

3. 'The bright-faced damsels,' i.e. intelligences derived from Idrís which have descended from the fourth heaven.

'Lissome,' i.e. inclining towards the phenomenal world, to replenish it. He means all realities that are connected with the phenomenal world, e.g. the Divine Names.

4. 'Who murder with their black eyes,' referring to the sciences of contemplation.

5. 'Indian,' because India is the place where Adam fell, and there the fountains of wisdom which were in Adam first gushed forth.

[1] The author expressly says in his commentary that وعد (to promise) has here the meaning of اوعد (to threaten). This is a defiance of the established usage, just as لا تَفِ (for لا تَفي) is a violation of grammar.

6. 'Pure silk,' i.e. undyed, in reference to her being removed from all contamination.

'Anointed with *nadd*,' i.e. with mixed perfumes. He means that she is invested with Divine qualities.

9. 'She loves not that which I love,' i.e. she is not limited by the will of anyone, and if it happens that her will is in accord with mine, that is due to the effect produced by her upon me, not to the effect produced by me upon her.

'She does not fulfil,' etc., i.e. she is clement and forgiving.

10. 'Her plaited lock,' i.e. a chain of evidences and proofs.

'A black serpent,' referring to the science of the Divine majesty and awe.

11. He says that he is only afraid of missing the contemplation of his Beloved, and that he hesitated to follow her because he wished to acquire such Divine faculties as would enable him to face this manifestation.

XXIII

1. At dawn they alighted in Wádi 'l-'Aqíq after having traversed many a deep ravine,
2. And at daybreak they descried a cairn shining on the top of a mountain peak.
3. When the vulture desires to reach it he is unable, and the eggs of the *anúq* are below it.
4. Ornaments are set upon it: its foundations are lofty, like al-'Aqúq.
5. And they had written some lines which were communicated to them: 'Oh, who will help a forlorn and longing lover,
6. Who although his thought soars above this Arcturus, is trodden underfoot like burning ashes,[1]
7. And whose home is beside this Aquila, yet he has died in tears the death of the drowned?
8. His love hath delivered him to calamities in this place without a brother to befriend him.

[1] This translation of الحريق is conjectural.

9. Then, O ye who come to the waters of the well, and O ye who inhabit Wádi 'l-'Aqíq,
10. And O thou who seekest Medína to visit it, and O ye who travel on this road,
11 Look on us again with pity! for we were robbed, a little after dawn, a little before sunrise,
12. Of a bright-faced lissome damsel sweet of breath, diffusing a perfume like shredded musk,
13. Swaying drunkenly to and fro like the branches, fresh as raw silk,[1] which the winds have bent,
14. Shaking, like the hump of a stallion-camel, fearsome hips huge as sand-hills.
15. No censor blamed me for loving her, and my friend did not blame me for loving her.
16. If any censor had blamed me for loving her, my sobbing would have been my answer to him.
17. My desire is my troop of camels and my grief is my garment and my passion is my morning drink and my tears are my evening drink.'

Commentary

1. He describes pilgrims on the way to the Truth, travelling in themselves through the night of their bodily existence and stopping for rest at dawn, i.e. the boundary which divides the wisdom appertaining to the Divine realities that is deposited in the phenomenal world from the realities of the Spirits of Light, which are called allegorically the Heavenly Host (الملأ الاعلى). The travellers cause their camels, i.e. their aspirations, to halt in the Wádi 'l-'Aqíq, where pilgrims put on the garb of pilgrimage (احرام). This is the station of Muḥammadan sanctity (حرمة محمّدية).

2. 'A cairn,' i.e. a guide, namely, the spirit.

'A mountain peak,' i.e. the body.

[1] Sir Charles Lyall has suggested that الشقيق should be rendered 'red poppies', but the commentary runs: الشقيق هو الحرير الخام لم يداخله (MS. يدخله) صنعة الآدمى يقول انها على ما هى عليه.

3. 'The vulture,' i.e. the spirit of the intermediate world (الروح البرزخي), which is nearer than any other of the ruling spirits (الارواح المدبّرة) to the Heavenly Host.

'The *anúq*,' which lays its eggs in the loftiest and most inaccessible places.

4. 'Ornaments,' i.e. the manifestation of the Divine qualities. In Bodl. (Uri) 1276, the commentary states that al-'Aqúq is said to be a great castle on the top of a high mountain.

7. 'And whose home,' etc., i.e. this station, notwithstanding its sublimity, is veiled by various sorts of revealed knowledge, belonging to the class of love, from this person who abides there, so that he is caused to pass away from the contemplation of himself in this centre of manifestation.

9. 'The waters of the well,' i.e. the life acquired from good works, viz. the life of knowledge (حياة العلم), in reference to Kor. vi, 122 : '*Shall he who was dead and whom we restored to life . . . ?*'

10. 'On this road,' i.e. the right way (الصراط المستقيم), in reference to Kor. vi, 154.

11. 'A little before sunrise,' i.e. the hour of the ascent that succeeds the Divine descent into the terrestrial heaven, which descent occurs in the last third of the night.

12. 'A bright-faced lissome damsel,' i.e. the Essential attribute which is his object of desire. She is called 'lissome' because of her descent towards us, yet from it nothing is derived that can be grasped by knowledge or understanding or imagination.

'Diffusing a perfume,' etc., i.e. leaving Divine impressions in the hearts of her worshippers.

13. 'Swaying drunkenly,' in reference to the station of bewilderment (حيرة).

'Which the winds have bent,' i.e. the aspirations (الهمم) by seeking her cause her to incline, as God says, 'If anyone comes a span nearer to Me, I will come a cubit nearer to him.'

14. This verse refers to the infinite bounties, spiritual and other, which God has heaped upon His servants.

15. Inasmuch as she is like the sun, which is common to all, she does not excite jealousy.

16. 'My sobbing,' i.e. my ecstasy would make me deaf to his reproaches.

17. 'My desire is my troop of camels,' which bear me to my Beloved.

XXIV

The author says: A dervish recited to me the following verse, to which I knew not any brother—

> 'Everyone who hopes for thy bounty receives copious showers thereof; thy lightning never breaks its promise of rain except with me.'

I admired its application and pursued its meaning, and I composed some verses in the same rhyme, including this verse among them on account of its perfection, and I said in answer to that dervish (may God have mercy on him!) as follows:—

1. Halt by the ruined abodes at La'la' and mourn for our loved ones in that wilderness.
2. Halt by thy dwelling-places and call to them, wondering at their loneliness, with exquisite lamentation.
3. 'Beside thy *bán* tree I have seen many a one like myself plucking the fruit of comely forms and the roses of a verdant meadow.
4. Everyone who hopes for thy bounty receives copious showers thereof; thy lightning never breaks its promise of rain except with me.'
5. She said, 'Yes; there hath been that meeting in the shadow of my boughs in the most plenteous spot,
6. When my lightning was one of the lightnings of smiling mouths; but to-day my lightning is the flash of this brilliant stone.
7. Reproach, then, a fate which we had no means of averting: what is the fault of the camping-place at La'la'?'
8. I excused her when I heard her speech and how she was complaining even as I complain with a sorrowful heart,

9. And I asked her, when I saw her demesne, through which the four winds sweep at night,
10. 'Did their winds tell thee where they rested at noontide?' She said, 'Yes; they rested at Dhát al-Ajra',
11. Where the white tents are radiant with those rising suns within.'

COMMENTARY

1. 'The ruined abodes,' i.e. the vestiges of the dwelling-places of the Divine Names in the hearts of gnostics.

'In that wilderness,' i.e. in his empty heart.

3. 'Plucking the fruit of comely forms,' i.e. the manifold knowledge of the Divine Self-subsistence (القيّومية), with which, according to our doctrine, it is possible to be invested. This investiture (تخلّق) is a matter of dispute amongst the Ṣúfís; Ibn Junayd al-Ifríqí and his followers consider that it is not correct.

'The roses of a verdant meadow,' referring to the station of Shame (الحيا), which results from meditation and contemplation.

4. 'Thy lightning never breaks its promise,' etc., i.e. through the lack of Divine favour (لعدم العناية). He also indicates that he himself is in a lofty station which was not reached by any of his peers, because the lightning is a *locus* of manifestation for the Essence, and from this *locus* the soul of the seer gains no knowledge, inasmuch as it is a manifestation devoid of material form.

6. 'When my lightning,' etc., i.e. that manifestation took place in a lovely form, but my manifestation to thee is formless and inanimate (جماديّة) and is not determined by love and passion.

11. 'The white tents,' in reference to the veils of light which are drawn over the splendours of the face of God.

XXV

1. O grief for my heart, O grief! O joy for my mind, O joy!
2. In my heart the fire of passion is burning, in my mind the full moon of darkness hath set.

3. O musk! O full moon! O bough of the sand-hills! How green is the bough, how bright the moon, how sweet the musk!
4. O smiling mouth whose bubbles I loved! and O saliva in which I tasted white honey!
5. O moon that appeared to us veiled in a red blush of shame upon thy cheek!
6. Had she removed her veil, it would have been a torment, and on this account she veiled herself.
7. She is the morning sun rising in a heaven, she is the bough of the sand-hills planted in a garden.
8. Fear made me watch her incessantly while I watered the bough with falling rain.
9. If she riseth, she will be a wonder to mine eye, or if she setteth she will be a cause of my death.
10. Since Beauty bound on her head a diadem of unwrought gold, I am in love with gold that has been wrought.
11. If Iblís had seen in Adam the brilliance of her face, he would not have refused to worship him.
12. If Idrís had seen the lines that Beauty limned on her cheeks, then he would never have written.
13. If Bilqís had seen her couch, the throne and the pavement would not have occurred to her mind.
14. O *sarḥ* tree of the valley and O *bán* tree of the thicket, deliver to us of your perfume, by means of the zephyr,
15. A musky odour which exhales its fragrance to us from the flowers of thy lowlands or the flowers of the hills.
16. O *bán* tree of the valley, show us a branch or some twigs that can be compared with *her* tenderness!
17. The zephyr's breeze tells of the time of youth spent at Ḥájir or Miná or Qubá,
18. Or at the sand-hills and where the vale bends beside the guarded pasture or at La'la', where the gazelles come to browse.
19. Do not wonder, do not wonder, do not wonder at an Arab passionately fond of the coy beauties,

20. Who, whenever a turtle-dove moans, is thrilled by the remembrance of his beloved and passes away.

COMMENTARY

1. 'O grief for my heart': he fears that the anguish of love will destroy this body by the mediation of which he has acquired the Divine sciences. Although most souls desire to be stripped thereof and to return to their elemental world, yet in the opinion of profound theosophists abstraction from the body should only be sought through ecstasy and self-annihilation (حالاً وفناءً), not by dissolving the connexion of body and soul.

'O joy for my mind,' because the mind is the *locus* in which the Truth is contemplated.

2. 'The full moon of darkness hath set': in reference to the Tradition, 'Ye shall see your Lord as ye see the moon on the night when she is full.'

'Darkness,' i.e. the invisible world. He describes the moon as having set in the sensible world and risen in his mind.

3. 'O musk,' i.e. breathing Divine mercy.

'O full moon,' because her light is borrowed from the Light of God, and because she is a mirror for Him who manifests Himself in her.

'O bough of the sand-hills,' referring to the quality of Self-subsistence (القيّوميّة).

'How green is the bough!' i.e. clothed with Divine Names.

4. 'Bubbles': as water is the source of all life, the bubbles signify the sciences of Divine mercy which appear from the Divine Life when the breaths (of mercy) flow.

'Saliva,' i.e. sciences of communion and converse and speech which leave a delicious taste in the heart.

5. God is described as bashful (حيى) in an Apostolic Tradition.

6. 'Had she removed her veil,' etc.: according to the Tradition, 'God hath seventy thousand veils of light and darkness; if He were to remove them, the splendours of His face would consume all that His sight perceives.' Therefore

He keeps Himself veiled in mercy to us, in order that our substance may survive, for in the survival of the substance of phenomenal being the Divine Presence and its lovely Names are manifested, and this is the beauty of phenomenal being; if it perished, thou wouldst not know, since all kinds of knowledge are divulged by means of forms and bodies.

7. 'In a heaven,' referring to the form in which the manifestation takes place. The form varies according to the variety of beliefs and cognitions; and this is what is called 'transformation' (التبدّل والتحوّل فى الصور). Some gnostics, e.g. Qaḍíb al-Bán, attain to this station in a sensible form. Its spiritual form comprises all the mystical states (احوال) of mankind.

'The bough of the sand-hills,' the quality of Self-subsistence in the garden of the Divine Names.

'Planted' refers to the investiture (تخلّق) with this quality, a doctrine which is contrary to that of Ibn Junayd and others. We agree, however, as to its realization (تحقّق), although I deny the possibility of realizing anything which cannot be an object of such investiture, since it is not to be apprehended by feeling (ذوق): it may be known symbolically, but not emotionally.

8. 'Fear made me watch her,' i.e. in fear of being veiled from her I began to behold her in everything and before everything, regarding everything as depending on her and immanent (in God) before its creation.

'I watered the bough,' in order that the Divine sciences which it contains might bear fruit in me.

9. 'She will be a wonder,' for it is wonderful that Man in his abasement should apprehend God in His glory.

10. 'Beauty,' i.e. a *locus* of ocular manifestation in the station of severance (التفرقة), in which Man is discriminated from God.

'Unwrought gold,' referring to her freedom from contact with phenomena.

'Gold that has been wrought': gold denotes the quality

of perfection which is attained by completing the series of stations. It is described as wrought, because God's manifestation to us by means of ourselves is actual, whereas His manifestation to us by means of Himself is not.

12. Idrís typifies the speculative theologian.

13. 'Her couch,' i.e. her lofty degree.

'Her mind': با for بال (mind), because ب (بآء), the second letter of the alphabet, signifies Universal Reason, which is the second category of Being.

15. 'From the flowers of thy lowlands,' i.e. the station of Divine Revelation (التنزيل الالهى) which descends in the Sunna of the Apostle and in the revealed scriptures.

'The flowers of the hills,' i.e. the most inaccessible veil of the Divine glory.

16. Man seeks God in want and in desire to receive, whereas God seeks Man in wealth and in desire to give.

17. 'The zephyr's breeze,' etc., i.e. the sciences wafted into the heart from the revelation and manifestation of God in diverse stations.

18. 'At the sand-hills,' i.e. the mount of Vision.

'Where the vale bends,' i.e. the station of Mercy, which allows the human essence to subsist 'beside the guarded pasture', i.e. at the manifestation of the Divine essence.

'At La'la',' i.e. in the frenzy of love.

19. Do not wonder at a thing which yearns for its original home.

20. 'A turtle-dove,' i.e. the soul of a gnostic like himself, whose sublime utterance excites in him a longing for God.

XXVI

1. In the valley-curve between the two stony tracts is the trysting-place. Make our camels kneel, for here is the journey's end.
2. Do not seek (any other spot) and do not call after this, 'O Báriq! O Ḥájir! O Thahmad!'
3. And play as friendly full-breasted damsels played, and pasture as shy gazelles pastured

4. In a meadow whose flies sang and hummed and a warbling bird there answered them joyously.
5. Soft were its sides and soft its breeze, and the clouds were flashing and thundering,
6. And the raindrops were descending from the crevices of the clouds like tears shed by a passionate lover because he is parted from her he loves.
7. And drink the pure essence of its wine with its intoxication, and listen rapturously to a singer who chanteth there:
8. 'O the pure wine that in Adam's time related concerning the Garden of Eden an authentic tradition!
9. Verily, the fair women scattered it from the water of their mouths like musk and the virgins bestowed it on us without stint.'

Commentary

1. 'In the valley-curve between the two stony tracts,' i.e. in the place where Divine favours are bestowed on the soul which is the *locus* of an Essential manifestation.

'The trysting-place,' referring either to the station of Faith or to God's taking a covenant from the souls of mankind.

'The journey's end,' i.e. the mystery of everlasting life.

2. 'Do not seek,' etc., in accordance with the Tradition, 'There is no mark beyond God.'

3. 'And play,' etc., referring to the various states of this gnostic in which he is transported from one Divine Name to another. 'Full-breasted damsels' and 'shy gazelles' refer to the abstruse sciences of pure unification.

4. 'In a meadow,' i.e. the Divine Presence, together with the Holy Names contained in it.

'Flies,' i.e. subtle spirits.

'A warbling bird,' i.e. the human soul, in respect of the forms with which it is endued in every sphere and station.

5. 'Were flashing and thundering,' in reference to the two states, viz. contemplation and interlocution (مشاهدة وخطاب) Cf. Kor. ii, 206, and the Tradition, 'God was in a dense cloud; there was no air above Him or below Him.'

6. 'The raindrops,' i.e. manifold sorts of Divine knowledge.

7. 'The pure essence of its wine,' i.e. spiritual meanings and Divine sciences, which fill the heart with delight.

'A singer,' i.e. the voice (الناطق) produced by the universal praise (الذكر الجامع); the human soul hears it in its essence and is enraptured.

8. 'The Garden of Eden,' i.e. this wine is derived from the Presence which comes to dwell in the souls of gnostics at the time of nurture (في اوان التربية).

9. 'The fair women,' i.e. the Divine Names.

'From the water of their mouths,' i.e. from the station of speech and expression.

'The virgins,' i.e. from the station of shame, referring to contemplation.

XXVII

1. O ancient temple, there hath risen for you a light that gleams in our hearts.
2. I complain to thee of the deserts which I crossed, where I let my tears flow unchecked,
3. Taking no joy in rest at dawn or dusk, continuing from morn to morn and passing from eve to eve.
4. Truly, the camels, even if they suffer from footsoreness, journey by night and make haste in their journey.
5. These beasts of burden carried us to you with eager desire, though they did not hope to attain thereby.
6. They traversed wildernesses and wellnigh rainless lands, impelled by passion, but they did not therefore complain of fatigue.
7. They did not complain of the anguish of love, and 'tis I who complain of fatigue. Indeed, I have claimed something absurd.

Commentary

1. 'O ancient temple,' i.e. the gnostic's heart which contains the reality of the Truth.

'There hath risen for you,' etc., i.e. the light in the heart (which is the centre of the body) seeks to rise from its source and convey to the members of the body the Divine realities. In this station a man sees by God, hears by God, speaks by God, and moves by God.

2. 'The deserts which I crossed,' i.e. the mortifications and austerities which I suffered.

4. 'The camels,' i.e. the aspirations. He means that they do not cease from seeking, although exhausted by the difficulty of their quest. They are exhausted because the proofs supplied by the understanding are unable to lead them to the Divine reality.

7. 'I have claimed something absurd,' i.e. I pretend to love God, while complaining of distress and fatigue, yet these 'beasts of burden', viz. my acts and thoughts which I control and govern, make no complaint.

XXVIII

1. Between al-Naqá and La'la' are the gazelles of Dhát al-Ajra',
2. Grazing there in a dense covert of tangled shrubs, and pasturing.
3. New moons never rose on the horizon of that hill
4. But I wished, from fear, that they had not risen.
5. And never appeared a flash from the lightning of that fire-stone
6. But I desired, for my feeling's sake, that it had not flashed.
7. O my tears, flow! O mine eye, cease not to shed tears!
8. O my sighs, ascend! O my heart, split!
9. And thou, O camel-driver, go slowly, for the fire is between my ribs.
10. From their copious flow through fear of parting my tears have all been spent,
11. So that, when the time of starting comes, thou wilt not find an eye to weep.
12. Set forth, then, to the valley of the curving sands, their abode and my death-bed—

13. There are those whom I love, beside the waters of al-Ajra'—
14. And call to them, 'Who will help a youth burning with desire, one dismissed,
15. Whose sorrows have thrown him into a bewilderment which is the last remnant of ruin ?
16. O moon beneath a darkness, take from him something and leave something,
17. And bestow on him a glance from behind yonder veil,
18. Because he is too weak to apprehend the terrible beauty,
19. Or flatter him with hopes, that perchance he may be revived or may understand.
20. He is a dead man between al-Naqá and La'la'.'
21. For I am dead of despair and anguish, as though I were fixed in my place.
22. The East Wind did not tell the truth when it brought cheating phantoms.
23. Sometimes the wind deceives when it causes thee to hear what is not (really) heard.

COMMENTARY

1. 'Between al-Naqá and La'la',' etc., i.e. between the hill of white musk, on which is the vision of God, and the place of frenzied love for Him, are diverse sorts of knowledge connected with the stations of abstraction (التجريد).

2. 'In a dense covert of tangled shrubs,' i.e. the world of phenomenal admixture and interdependence.

3. 'New moons,' i.e. Divine manifestations.

4. 'From fear,' i.e. from fear that the beholder might pass away in himself from himself, and that his essence might perish, whereas his object is to continue subsistent through God and for God; or from fear that he should imagine the manifestation to be according to the essential nature of God in Himself (which is impossible), and not according to the nature of the recipient. The former belief, which involves the comprehension (احاطة) of God by the person to whom the manifestation is made, agrees with the

doctrine of some speculative theologians, who maintain that our knowledge of God and Gabriel's knowledge of Him and His knowledge of Himself are the same. How far is this from the truth!

5. 'A flash from the lightning of that fire-stone,' i.e. an inanimate, phenomenal, and earthly manifestation.

9. 'O camel-driver,' i.e. the voice of God calling the aspirations to Himself.

'The fire,' i.e. the fire of love.

10–11. He says that his eyes have been melted away by the tears which he shed in anticipation of parting.

12. 'To the valley of the curving sands,' i.e. the station of mercy and tenderness.

'My death-bed,' because the Divine mercy causes him to pass away in bewilderment.

13. 'Beside the waters of al-Ajra'': because this mercy is the result of painful self-mortification (تجريع الغصص فى الرياضات والمجاهدات).

14. 'One dismissed,' i.e one who has come to himself again after contemplation, according to the tradition that God says, after having shown Himself to His servants in Paradise, 'Send them back to their pavilions.'

16. 'A darkness,' i.e. the forms in which the manifestation takes place.

'Take from him something,' etc., i.e. take from him whatever is related to himself, and leave whatever is not related to himself, so that only the Divine Spirit may remain in him.

21. 'For I am dead of despair and anguish,' i.e. I despair of attaining the reality of that which I seek, and I grieve for the time spent in a vain search for it.

'As though I were fixed in my place,' i.e. I cannot escape from my present state, inasmuch as it is without place, quantity, and quality, being purely transcendental (تنزّه وتجرّد).

22. 'Cheating phantoms,' i.e. the similes and images in which God, who has no like, is presented to us by the world of breaths (عالم الانفاس).

XXIX

1. May my father be the ransom of the boughs swaying to and fro as they bend, bending their tresses towards the cheeks!
2. Loosing plaited locks of hair; soft in their joints and bends;
3. Trailing skirts of haughtiness; clad in embroidered garments of beauty;
4. Which from modesty grudge to bestow their loveliness; which give old heirlooms and new gifts;
5. Which charm by their laughing and smiling mouths; whose lips are sweet to kiss;
6. Whose bare limbs are dainty; which have swelling breasts and offer choice presents;
7. Luring ears and souls, when they converse, by their wondrous witchery;
8. Covering their faces for shame, taking captive thereby the devout and fearing heart;
9. Displaying teeth like pearls, healing with their saliva one who is feeble and wasted;
10. Darting from their eyes glances which pierce a heart experienced in the wars and used to combat;
11. Making rise from their bosoms new moons which suffer no eclipse on becoming full;
12. Causing tears to flow as from rain-clouds, causing sighs to be heard like the crash of thunder.
13. O my two comrades, may my life-blood be the ransom of a slender girl who bestowed on me favours and bounties!
14. She established the harmony of union, for she is our principle of harmony: she is both Arab and foreign; she makes the gnostic forget.
15. Whenever she gazes, she draws against thee trenchant swords, and her front teeth show to thee a dazzling levin.
16. O my comrades, halt beside the guarded pasture of Ḥájir! Halt, halt, O my comrades,

17. That I may ask where their camels have turned, for I have plunged into places of destruction and death,
18. And scenes known to me and unknown, with a swift camel which complains of her worn hoofs and of deserts and wildernesses,
19. A camel whose flanks are lean and whose rapid journeying caused her to lose her strength and the fat of her hump,
20. Until I brought her to a halt in the sandy tract of Ḥájir and saw she-camels followed by young ones at al-Uthayl.
21. They were led by a moon of awful mien, and I clasped him to my ribs for fear that he should depart,
22. A moon that appeared in the circumambulation, and while he circumambulated me I was not circumambulating anyone except him.
23. He was effacing his footprints with the train of his robe, so that thou wouldst be bewildered even if thou wert the guide tracing out his track.

Commentary

1. 'My father,' i.e. Universal Reason.

'The boughs,' i.e. the Attributes which bear Divine knowledge to gnostics and mercifully incline towards them.

2. 'Locks of hair,' i.e. hidden sciences and mysteries. They are called 'plaited' in allusion to the various degrees of knowledge.

'Soft,' in respect of their graciously inclining to us.

'In their joints and bends,' in reference to the conjunction of real and phenomenal qualities.

3. 'Trailing skirts,' etc., because of the loftiness of their rank.

'Clad in embroidered garments,' etc., i.e. appearing in diverse beautiful shapes.

4. 'Which from modesty,' etc., referring to the Tradition, 'Do not bestow wisdom except on those who are worthy of it, lest ye do it a wrong,' since contemplation is not vouchsafed to everyone.

'Old heirlooms,' i.e. knowledge demonstrated by proofs derived from another.

'New gifts,' i.e. knowledge of which the proof is bestowed by God and occurs to one's own mind as the result of sound reflection.

8. 'Covering their faces for shame,' i.e. they are ashamed to reveal themselves to those whose hearts are generally occupied with something other than God, viz. the ordinary believers described in Kor. ix, 103.

9. 'Teeth like pearls,' i.e. the sciences of Divine majesty.

10. 'Experienced in the wars,' etc., i.e. able to distinguish the real from the phenomenal in the similitudes presented to the eye.

11. 'From their bosoms,' i.e. from the Divine attributes.

'New moons,' i.e. a manifestation in the horizon (تجلٍّ أُفُقى).

'Which suffer no eclipse,' i.e. they are not subject to any natural lust that veils them from the Divine Ideas.

13. 'A slender girl,' i.e. the single, subtle, and essential knowledge of God.

14. 'She established the harmony of union,' i.e. this knowledge concentrated me upon myself and united me with my Lord.

'Arab,' i.e. it caused me to know myself from myself.

'Foreign,' i.e. it caused me to know myself from God, because the Divine knowledge is synthetic (اجمالية) and does not admit of analysis except by means of comparison; and since comparison is impossible, therefore analysis is impossible; whence it follows that synthesis also is impossible, and I only use the latter term in order to convey to the reader's intelligence a meaning that is not to be apprehended save by immediate feeling and intuition.

'Forget,' i.e. his knowledge and himself.

15. 'A dazzling levin,' i.e. a manifestation of the Essence in the state of beauty and joy.

16. 'O my comrades': he means his understanding and his faith.

17. 'Their camels,' i.e. the aspirations which carry the sciences and subtle essences of man to their goal.

18. 'A swift camel,' i.e. an aspiration in himself.

19. 'Whose rapid journeying,' etc., i.e. this aspiration was connected with many aspects of plurality which disappeared in the course of its journey towards Unity.

20. 'In the sandy tract of Ḥájir,' i.e. a state which enabled me to discriminate between phenomena and prevented me from regarding anything except what this state revealed to me.

'She-camels followed by young ones,' i.e. original sciences from which other sciences are derived.

21. 'A moon of awful mien,' i.e. a manifestation of Divine majesty in the heart.

23. 'His footprints,' i.e. the evidences which He adduced as a clue to Himself.

'The train of his robe,' i.e. His uniqueness and incomparability.

'So that thou wouldst be bewildered,' i.e. our knowledge of Him is ignorance and bewilderment and helplessness. He says this in order that gnostics may recognize the limits of their knowledge of God.

XXX

1. In the tamarisk groves of al-Naqá is a flock of *qaṭá* birds over whom Beauty has pitched a tent,
2. And in the midst of the deserts of Iḍam are camels which graze beside them and gazelles.
3. O my two friends, stop and beg speech of the relics of an abode which has become ruined after them,
4. And mourn for the heart of a youth who left it on the day when they departed, and weep and wail.
5. Perchance it may tell whither they were bound, to the sands of the guarded pasture or to Qubá.
6. They saddled the camels and I knew not whether 'twas from my heedlessness or because mine eye was dull.
7. 'Twas neither that nor this, but 'twas only a frenzy of love which overwhelmed me.

8. O thoughts that fled and dispersed in pursuit of them like the bands of Sabá!
9. I hailed every wind that blows, crying, 'O North wind! O South wind! O East wind!
10. Have ye any knowledge of what I feel? Anguish hath befallen me on account of their departure.'
11. The East wind gave me its news delivered by the *shíḥ* plants which received it from the hill-flowers,
12. Saying, 'Whosoever is sick of the malady of passion, let him be diverted by the tales of love.'
13. Then it said, 'O North wind, tell him the like of what I have told him, or something more wonderful.
14. Then do thou, O South wind, relate the like of what I have related to him or something more sweet.'
15. The North wind said, 'I have a joy which the North wind shares with the South wind:
16. Every evil is good in the passion which they inspire, and my torment is sweetened by their approval.'
17. To what end, therefore, and on what ground and for what cause dost thou complain of the sorrow and sickness?
18. And when they promise you aught, you see that its lightning gives a false promise of rain.
19. The Invisible fashioned on the sleeve of the cloud a golden embroidery of the lightning's splendour,
20. And its tears poured from it upon the middle of its cheek-balls and kindled a fierce flame.
21. She is a rose that springs up from tears, a narcissus that sheds a marvellous shower.
22. And when thou wouldst fain gather her, she lets down, to conceal herself, a scorpion-like tress on each side of her temples.
23. The sun rises when she smiles. O Lord, how bright are these bubbles on her teeth!
24. Night appears when she lets fall her black, luxuriant, and tangled hair.
25. The bees compete with one another whenever she spits. O Lord, how sweet is that coolness!

26. And whenever she bends she shows to us a (fruitful) branch, or when she gazes her looks are drawn swords.
27. How long wilt thou talk amorously at the sand-hill of Ḥájir, O son of al-'Arabí, to the coy beauties?
28. Am not I an Arab? and therefore I love the fair women and am fond of the coy beauties.
29. I care not whether my passion rises with me or sets, if only she be there.
30. Whenever I say 'Will ye not?' they say, 'Wilt not thou?' and whenever I say, 'May not I?' they say, 'He refuses.'
31. And whenever they go to the upland or to the lowland, I cross the desert in haste to search for them.
32. My heart is the Sámirí of the time: as often as it sees the footprints it seeks the golden one that was turned to gold.
33. And whenever they rise or set, it goes like Dhu 'l-Qarnayn in quest of the means (of reaching them).
34. How oft did we cry out in hope of union! How oft did we cry out in fear of parting!
35. O sons of az-Zawrá, this is a moon that appeared among you and set in me.
36. By God, it is the source of my grief. How often do I exclaim behind it, 'Alas!'
37. Woe is me, woe is me for a youth who, whenever a dove warbles, is made to vanish!

COMMENTARY

1. 'In the tamarisk groves,' etc., i.e. in the grove of the white hill are sciences which are the offspring of veracity, in reference to the proverb, 'More veracious than the *qaṭá*.'

2. 'The deserts of Idam,' i.e. the stations of abstraction and isolation (للتجريد والتفريد).

'Camels,' i.e. sciences with which our souls are familiar.

'Gazelles,' i.e. abstruse sciences.

3. 'O my two friends,' i.e. his understanding and his faith.

5. 'The sands of the guarded pasture,' referring to the endurance of anguish (تجرّع الغصص) caused by separation in a station remote from phenomenal being and inaccessible.

'Qubá,' i.e. the station of repose, for the Prophet used to alight there every Sabbath.

6. 'The camels,' i.e. the aspirations on which our hearts ride.

7. ''Twas only a frenzy of love,' etc., i.e. my preoccupation with love for Him veiled me from Himself.

13–14. The East wind bestows on him the knowledge of 'God created Adam after His own image', the South wind bestows on him the knowledge of the companions of the right hand (اصحاب اليمين, Kor. lvi, 89), and the North wind bestows on him the knowledge of the favourites of God (المقرّبون, Kor. lvi, 87), which is the station between prophecy and saintship and is attained only by the nonpareils (الافراد), of whom al-Khaḍir is one, as the Koran bears witness. Abú Ḥámid (al-Ghazálí) denies the existence of this station, because he never reached or knew it, and he imagines that those Saints who advance beyond the rank of the *ṣiddíqs* have fallen into prophecy and have acted irreverently, but such is not the case. The station to which I refer lies between the position of the *ṣiddíq* and that of the Prophet. It is indicated by the mystery which made an impression on the heart of the greatest *ṣiddíq*, Abú Bakr (السرّ الذى وقع اى وقر فى صدره).

16. When the lover passes away from his own desire, every evil becomes good to him, because it is the will and desire of his Beloved.

18. 'Its lightning gives a false promise of rain': a manifestation of the Essence produces nothing in the heart, inasmuch as it cannot be apprehended or confined by any phenomenal object. In this respect it differs from the manifestation in forms in the world of similitudes, for the seer apprehends the form of that which is manifested to him and interprets it.

19. 'On the sleeve of the cloud,' referring to Kor. ii, 206.

The cloud is the heart which clothes, i.e. contains, God. The sleeve represents the hand which takes the pledge of fealty to Him. The author describes a manifestation of the Essence behind the veil of phenomena, a manifestation due to the fact profoundly realized by a servant of God, that God created Adam in His image.

20. 'And its tears,' etc., i.e. diverse sorts of evidentiary knowledge poured into the gardens of the Divine hearts and produced an overwhelming sense of awe and majesty.

21. 'A narcissus,' i.e. a vision that imparts incomprehensible knowledge.

23. 'The sun rises,' i.e. sciences appear which are connected with the Quṭb and upon which the universe depends.

24. She reveals to the hearts of gnostics mysterious love.

25. When this gnostic feels in himself a Divine realization so that he attains to the station indicated in the Tradition, 'I am his ear and his eye,' his speech becomes pure Truth and absolute Revelation, and the hearts of his disciples receive from him knowledge in the same way as the bees receive honey from God (Kor. xvi, 70).

26. As the winds sway the bough, so the gnostic's aspiration causes God to incline mercifully towards him.

27. 'At the sand-hill of Ḥájir,' i.e. the white hill, well-known to the Ṣúfís, on which it is impossible for anyone to set foot. He says, 'Why dost thou not occupy thyself with making ready for the gifts bestowed by this high station, in order that no thought of "the coy beauties", i.e. contemplation and bewilderment, may occur to thee?'

28. He answers: 'The beauties which I seek are the offspring of the original fiat whence we came forth. I am an Arab (عربى) and therefore I love the coy beauties (العُرُب), i.e. do not blame me for acting as I am prompted by what in me is original and real.'

29. 'I care not,' etc., i.e. I am not limited by stations and degrees, but only by her, so that wherever she is I am.

30. When I say to the mediums and veils, 'Will you not consider my case with her, that perchance I may win of

her such delight as other ecstatics have enjoyed?' they answer: 'Wilt not thou consider our faces how they are turned towards thee and veiled from her?' i.e. secondary causes are merely an affliction and probation through which you must pass, but if you remain with them you will receive nothing except what their being can give, and you will be veiled from the object of your desire.

'May not I?' i.e. may not I attain to my Beloved?

'He refuses,' i.e. he excludes those who seek him by means of secondary causes. God is known only by means of God. The scholastic theologian says: 'I know God by that which He created,' and takes as his guide something that has no real relation to the object sought. He who knows God by means of phenomena, knows as much as those phenomena give to him and no more.

31. 'They go to the upland,' i.e. the Divine realities reveal themselves in imaginary bodies as Gabriel appeared in the form of Diḥya.

'To the lowland,' i.e. they reveal themselves, like the spirits of the prophets, in earthly bodies of the intermediate world.

32. 'As often as it sees the footprints,' etc.: cf. Kor. xx, 96. He says: 'There is in me an aspiration with which I revive those whom I regard with favour, and those whose growth is symmetrical, and those whose form is erect (I mean in the earthly pilgrimage), and those whose hearts are prepared to receive the overflowing grace of the spirit; and I breathe into them something of that which I have gained from that footprint, and they are revived thereby and are under my care.' He refers to the class of saints who have renounced the powers of 'control' (التصريف) which God bestowed upon them, for one who abides with the Primal Realities is more perfect in knowledge than one who is veiled by such Divine gifts. Abú Yazíd (al-Bisṭámí) said: 'It is not I whom they are touching, but it is a robe in which God clothed me: how, then, should I hinder them from that which belongs to another?' Whoever sees the

robe of honour which God conferred on the Black Stone, and knows the stone, will know what I mean. This was the station of Abú Yazíd and of my Shaykh, Abú Madyan.

34. How often did we beg for power over the spiritual states, so that we might rule them without fear of losing them!

35. 'O sons of az-Zawrá': az-Zawrá is a name of Baghdád, which is the residence of the Quṭb in the visible world. The author refers to those who are in the presence of the Quṭb and under his ægis (تحت دائرته).

'A moon,' etc., i.e. an essential manifestation which appeared among you through the existence of the Quṭb, and vanished in me, i.e. it is my inward being and mystery (باطني وسرّي). He makes himself to be one of the nonpareils (الافراد).

36. 'Behind it,' although it is within himself, indicating that it is not circumscribed (يشير الى عدم الاحاطة), but that it is with him in the category of additionals, as the Prophet said, 'O Lord, let me increase in knowledge.'

37. 'A dove,' i.e. the spirits of the intermediate world, the bearers of the inspiration that comes at the tinkling sound (الصلصلة), which is like the noise of a chain when it strikes a rock. They cause this heart to vanish, even as they themselves vanish on hearing that sound. Hence the Prophet said that this manner of inspiration was the most grievous to him, and he used to pass away from his senses, and wrap himself until it departed, after he had understood its meaning. A portion of this belongs to his (spiritual) heirs.

XXXI

1. A lightning-cloud gleamed at Dhát al-Aḍá, with light flashing over the plain thereof,
2. And the thunder of its secret converse cracked, and its rain-cloud let fall copious showers.
3. They called to one another: 'Make the camels kneel!' but they did not listen, and I in my passion cried out: 'O driver,

4. Alight here and abide, for I love one who is with you,
5. A woman, slender, lissome, of fresh beauty, for whom the heart of the sad lover is longing.'
6. The assembly is filled with fragrance at the mention of her, and every tongue utters her name.
7. And if her seat were a valley (but her throne is a high mountain),
8. The low ground would be made high by her: he who looks enviously shall never attain to that height.
9. By her is every desert peopled, and by her is every mirage transformed to abundant water,
10. And by her is every meadow made bright, and by her is every wine made clear.
11. My night is radiant with her face, and my day is dark with her hair.
12. The core of my heart, when the Cleaver shot it through with her arrows,
13. Was cloven by eyes which are accustomed to aim at the entrails, and none of their shafts misses the mark.
14. No owl in desert places, no ring-dove or croaking raven
15. Is more unlucky than a full-grown camel which they saddled, that it might carry away one whose beauty is surpassing,
16. And might leave at Dhát al-Aḍá a passionate lover slain, although in love of them he is true.

Commentary

1. 'A lightning-cloud.' i.e. a manifestation of the Essence.

'Dhát al-Aḍá,' in Tiháma, i.e. the station of abasement pertaining to exaltation, for God exalts those who humble themselves before Him.

'Light,' i.e. the light of exaltation.

4. 'Here,' i.e. beside one who seeks and loves you.

'One who is with you': he addresses the sciences imparted to him by this manifestation. Inasmuch as they are sought, not for their own sake but only for the sake of that on which they are dependent, he says that he desires to approach that by means of them.

5. 'A woman,' etc., i.e. a Divine attribute which manifested itself in the world of similitude.

7, 8. Her sublimity exalts everyone in whom she dwells.

'A high mountain,' i.e. the heart of the gnostic.

'He who looks enviously,' etc.: the Divine essence is unknowable.

9. 'Every desert,' i.e. every heart laid waste by forgetfulness of God.

10. 'Wine,' i.e. spiritual delight.

11. He says: 'I have gained knowledge of the invisible world from her hair, and knowledge of the visible world from her face, and my visible world produces her as an invisible being to the eye,' i.e. I have the power of appearing in different forms, like al-Khadir and some saints, e.g. Qadíb al-Bán.

12. 'The Cleaver,' i.e. God, in reference to Kor. vi, 95, 96.

13. 'Was cloven,' etc., i.e. by the sciences and manifestations of the Divine Ideas.

14–16. The most unlucky of all things is any ecstasy that intervenes between thee and this Divine attribute, for ecstasy takes possession of the heart, so that the mystery of the Almighty which was illuminated by this Essential Manifestation is left neglected and without power to retain that which has already been revealed to it.

XXXII

1. Our talk between al-Ḥadítha and al-Karkh recalls to me the period of youth and its prime.
2. I said to myself: 'After fifty years, when through long meditation I have become as weak as a young bird,
3. It recalls to me the neighbourhood of Sal' and Ḥájir, and brings to my mind the period of youth and its prime,
4. And the driving of the camels up hill and down dale, and

my kindling fire for them by rubbing the *'afár* and the *markh* together.'[1]

COMMENTARY

1–3. He says: 'Our praise of God (ذِكْر), telling of the Divine Revelation, recalls to me the time of pilgrimage in the station where the veils were rent and lifted from me by acts of devotion that produced spiritual feelings and aspirations of which I was unconscious, and brings me back from my present state of acting in unveiledness and without being conscious of consciousness to the former state of acting in which I was veiled.'

4. 'My kindling fire,' etc., i.e. the things generated by veiled secondary causes whereby the reality is doubly disguised.

XXXIII

1. I respond with diverse notes of grief to every cooing dove perched upon a bough in a grove.
2. She weeps for her mate without tears, but from my eyelids the tears of sorrow are streaming.
3. I say to her, when my eyelids have shed their abundant tears in token of my inward state,
4. 'Hast thou any knowledge of those whom I love, and did they rest at midday in the shadows of the branches?'

COMMENTARY

1. 'Every cooing dove,' i.e. subtle spiritual essences which appear in forms of the intermediate world.

2. 'From my eyelids,' etc.: because of my bodily existence.

4. 'Did they rest,' etc., i.e. did they show themselves in the shades of this natural organism, so that I may seek them there?

[1] *'Afár* and *markh* are the names of trees whose wood was used for this purpose.

XXXIV

1. At the hill among the mountains of Zarúd are haughty lions, by the looks of lissome women
2. Overthrown, though they were bred in the carnage of war. What match are the lions for the black eyes ?
3. The women's looks murdered them. How sweet are those looks from the daughters of kings !

Commentary

1. 'Haughty lions,' i.e. aspiring and courageous hearts. 'Lissome women,' i.e. the Divine Ideas.

3. 'From the daughters of kings,' referring to Kor. liv, 55: '*In the presence of a puissant king.*'

XXXV

1. Three full moons, unadorned by any ornament, went forth to at-Tan'ím with veiled faces.
2. They unveiled shining faces like suns and cried with a loud voice 'Labbayka', visiting the holy shrines.
3. And they approached, walking slowly as the *qaṭá* birds walk, in gowns of striped Yemen cloth.

Commentary

1. Three Divine Names went forth from the Divine Presence to at-Tan'ím, desiring to manifest their traces, i.e. their bliss (نعيم) consists in such manifestation. 'With veiled faces,' lest anyone who was unable to endure the sight of their splendour should behold them and perish.

2. 'They unveiled,' i.e. in the heart that was prepared to receive them.

'The holy shrines,' i.e. this noble heart.

3. 'In gowns of striped Yemen cloth,' i.e. graced by the subordinate Names which attended them like priests.

XXXVI

1. O earth of the Highland, mayst thou be a blessed highland ! May the rain-clouds water thee abundantly with shower on shower !

2. And may he who has greeted thee for fifty years greet thee once and twice and then once again !
3. I crossed every desert and wilderness to meet her, riding on the big-humped she-camel and the old dromedary,
4. Until the lightning shone from the direction of al-Ghaḍá, and its coming in the night has increased the passion that I felt before.

Commentary

1. 'O earth of the Highland,' i.e. the understanding in the corporeal world.

'The white clouds,' i.e. Divine Knowledge.

2. 'He who has greeted thee,' i.e. the Truth, which bestows spiritual gifts.

3. 'I crossed every desert and wilderness,' i.e. I suffered austerities and mortifications of the flesh.

'The big-humped she-camel,' i.e. the religious law.

'The old dromedary,' i.e. the matured and experienced mind.

4. 'The lightning,' i.e. the luminous radiance of the most inaccessible veil of the Divine glory.

'Al-Ghaḍá,' phenomenal existence.

'Coming in the night,' i.e. in the darkness of the phenomenal world.

XXXVII

1. O my two comrades, approach the guarded pasture and seek Najd and yonder sign that marks the way,
2. And come down to a well at the tents of the curving sand and beg shade of its *ḍál* and *salam* trees.
3. And whenever ye come to the valley of Miná—for then ye have come to that in which is my heart's being—
4. Deliver to all who dwell there the greetings of love from me, or only say, 'Peace be with you !'
5. And hearken what they will reply, and tell how one who is heartsick
6. Complains of the ardours of love, while he is hiding nothing, seeking information, and asking questions.

COMMENTARY

1. 'O my two comrades,' i.e. his understanding and his faith.

'The guarded pasture,' i.e. the veiled glory of God.

'Najd,' i.e. sublime knowledge.

'Yonder sign,' i.e. inductive knowledge.

2. 'A well,' i.e. the source of eternal life.

'At the tents of the curving sand,' i.e. in the presence of Divine mercy.

'Beg shade,' etc., i.e. seek delight in the knowledge that bewilders the intellect and is exempt from all limitation.

3. 'The valley of Miná,' i.e. the abodes of the Heavenly Host and of the Divine Names assembled for the purpose of manifestation.

4. 'Or only say,' etc., i.e. if they are not pleased to receive my greetings, then make no mention of me.

6. 'Asking questions,' i.e. touching the malady with which he is smitten, viz. the obstacles that hinder him from attaining to the object of his desire, notwithstanding that love has intoxicated his whole being.

XXXVIII

1. The dearest place on God's earth to me after Ṭayba and Mecca and the Farther Temple is the city of Baghdán.[1]
2. How should I not love the (City of) Peace, since I have there an Imám who is the guide of my religion and my reason and my faith ?
3. 'Tis the home of a daughter of Persia, one whose gestures are subtle and whose eyelids are languid.
4. She greets and revives those whom she killed with her looks, and she conferred the best (gift) after beauty and beneficence.

COMMENTARY

1. 'Ṭayba' (Medina), i.e. the station of Yathrib from which they return with utter failure to attain to true knowledge of the most glorious God, as Abú Bakr said, 'perception is

[1] Baghdán is one of the seven various spellings of Baghdád.

the incapacity to achieve perception.' This involves seeing God in everything.

'Mecca,' i.e. the perfect heart which contains the Truth.

'The Farther Temple' (Jerusalem), i.e. the station of holiness and purity.

'Baghdán,' i.e. Baghdád, because it is the abode of the Quṭb, in whom is the perfect manifestation of the form of the Divine presence.

3. 'A daughter of Persia,' i.e. a form of foreign wisdom (حكمة عجمية), connected with Moses, Jesus, Abraham, and other foreigners of the same class.

'Whose eyelids are languid,' i.e. she is tender and merciful.

4. 'The best (gift) after beauty and beneficence': Gabriel said, 'Beneficence (الاحسان) consists in thy worshipping God as though thou wert seeing Him,' and he added, 'for if thou seest Him not, yet He sees thee.' Hence 'the best gift' after beneficence is God's vision of thee.

XXXIX

1. My soul be the ransom of fair-complexioned and coy virgins who played with me as I was kissing the Pillar and the Stone!
2. When thou art lost in pursuit of them, thou wilt find no guide but in their scent, the sweetest of traces.
3. No moonless night darkened o'er me but I remembered them and journeyed in moonlight.
4. Only when I walk in their company of riders does the night seem to me like the sun in the morning.
5. My love urged me to dalliance with one of them, a beauty who hath no sister in humankind.
6. If she unveils her mouth, she will show to thee what sparkles like the sun in unchanging radiance.
7. The whiteness of her forehead is the sun's, the blackness of the hair on her brow is the night's: most wondrous of forms is she—a sun and a night together!
8. Through her we are in daylight during the night and in a night of hair at noon.

Commentary

1. 'Virgins,' i.e. Divine sciences embodied in the world of similitude.

'As I was kissing,' etc., i.e. in the station of Divine allegiance (المبايعة الالهيّة).

2. 'Their scent,' i.e. their traces in the hearts of the gnostics who know them.

3. 'No moonless night,' i.e. the darkness of ignorance or bewilderment.

7. 'The blackness of the hair on her brow,' i.e. the mysterious sciences of which she is the bearer, e.g. the Traditions respecting assimilation (التشبيه).

8. 'We are in daylight during the night,' etc., i.e. in the essence of the case God's invisibility is His visibility, and His visibility is His invisibility, if we regard Him and not our own reason.

XL

1. Between Adhri'át and Buṣrá a maid of fourteen rose to my sight like a full moon.
2. She was exalted in majesty above Time and transcended it in pride and glory.
3. Every full moon, when it reaches perfection, suffers a waning that it may make a complete month,
4. Except this one: for she does not move through zodiacal signs nor double what is single.
5. Thou art a pyx containing blended odours and perfume, thou art a meadow producing spring-herbs and flowers.
6. Beauty reached in thee her utmost limit: another like thee is impossible.

Commentary

1. 'Between Adhri'át and Buṣrá': he mentions these places because they mark the farthest point reached by the Prophet in his Syrian journey.

'A maid of fourteen,' i.e. the perfect soul. Four is the

most perfect number, and ten consists of four numbers, viz. 1 + 2 + 3 + 4, and fourteen is 4 + 10.

4. 'Nor double what is single,' i.e. she is in the station of Unity and no one is joined with her, for she is not homogeneous with anything.

5. 'Blended odours and perfume,' i.e. Divine sciences and influences.

6. 'Beauty reached in thee her utmost limit,' as Abú Ḥámid (al-Ghazálí) said, 'A more beautiful world than this is not possible. Had it existed and had God kept it to Himself, He would have shown avarice which is incompatible with His liberality and weakness which is contradictory to His omnipotence.'

XLI

1. God save a bird on a *bán* tree, a bird that has revealed to me the true story
2. How the loved ones bound the saddles on their camels and then gat them away at dawn.
3. I journeyed—and in my heart for their sake was a blazing fire because of their departure—
4. Striving to outpace them in the darkness of the night, calling to them, and then following their track.
5. I had no guide in pursuing them except a perfumed breath of their love.
6. The women raised the curtain, the darkness became light, and the camels journeyed on because of the moonshine.
7. Then I let my tears pour in front of the camels, and the riders said, 'When did this river flow?'
8. And were unable to cross it. I said, 'My tears rolled in streams.'
9. 'Tis as though the thunderclaps at the gleam of the lightnings and the passing of the clouds at the fall of rain
10. Were the palpitation of hearts at the flash of teeth and the flow of tears for travellers who rode away.

11. O thou who likenest the lissomeness of the tall forms (of the loved ones) to the softness of the fresh verdant bough,
12. If thou hadst reversed the comparison, as I have done, thou wouldst have taken a sound view;
13. For the softness of the branches is like the lissomeness of the tall forms, and the rose of the meadow is like the rosy blush of shame.

Commentary

1. 'A bird on a *bán* tree,' i.e. the Prophet's spirit in his body.

'The true story,' i.e. the Tradition concerning the descent of God to the terrestrial heaven.

2. 'How the loved ones,' etc., i.e. how God descended into the night of phenomenal forms and 'gat Him away at dawn', that is, manifested Himself in the intermediate world, which, like the dawn, is light mingled with darkness; for this manifestation is impure in comparison with the purity and holiness of the Godhead *per se*.

4. 'Following their track': he refers to the investiture with Divine qualities.

5. 'A perfumed breath,' alluding to the habit of guides, who on losing their way in desert places try to recover it by smelling the earth.

6. This verse refers to Kor. xxxiv, 22: '*when the terror shall be removed from their hearts,*' etc.

7. 'The riders,' i.e. the angels mentioned in Kor. ii, 206.

8. 'And were unable to cross it,' because these tears were shed in the grief of parting, and the Heavenly Host lack this emotion, for they are not veiled from God: hence they are not allowed to traverse this station.

11–13. The author says that, in accordance with the real relation subsisting between God and His creatures, they should be connected with Him, not He with them. Thus the supple bough should be compared to the form of the Divine Beloved and the rose to His cheeks, not *vice versâ*, as happens in those Traditions which attribute human qualities to God, although in reality He is the eternal source of such qualities and therefore incomparable.

XLII

1. O men of intelligence and understanding, I am distraught between the sun and the gazelles.
2. He who forgets Suhá is not forgetful, but he who forgets the sun is forgetful.
3. Let him offer himself to his herd, for gifts open the mouth to utter praise.
4. Verily, she is an Arab girl, belonging by origin to the daughters of Persia, yea, verily.
5. Beauty strung for her a row of fine pearly teeth, white and pure as crystal.
6. I boded ill from her unveiling, and at that moment her loveliness and splendour affrighted me.
7. From those twain I suffered two deaths: thus hath the Koran revealed her.
8. I said, 'Wherefore did thy unveiling affright me?' (She answered), 'Thy foes have trysted to attack thee when the sun shines.'
9. I said, 'I am in a guarded demesne of black hair that hides thee: let it fall at their coming.'
10. This poem of mine is without rhyme: I intend by it only Her.
11. The word 'Her' is my aim, and for Her sake I am not fond of bartering except (with) 'Give and take' (*há wa-há*).[1]

Commentary

1. 'Between the sun and the gazelles,' referring to Kor. lxv, 12: '*The Divine command descendeth between them*' (viz. the heavens and the earth).

2. The heedless man is not he who neglects what is

[1] The meaning of the last hemistich is obscure. Possibly ها وها was a formula used in completing a bargain.

invisible, like the star Suhá, but he who neglects what is visible and manifest, like the sun.

3. 'Let him offer himself to his herd,' etc., i.e. let him sacrifice himself for the sake of those whom he loves, and then they will praise him.

4. 'An Arab girl,' i.e. one of the Muḥammadan kinds of knowledge.

'Belonging by origin to the daughters of Persia': for the foreign and barbarous idiom (العُجْمة) is more ancient than the Arabic (العربيّة).

6. 'I boded ill from her unveiling': when a woman unveiled herself to an Arab with no particular motive, he used to regard it as a sign that she was unlucky to him, and he used to be afraid in consequence.

7. 'Two deaths,' i.e. dying to (becoming unconscious of) others, and dying to himself, so that he remained with her in virtue of her, not in virtue of himself.

'Thus hath the Koran revealed her,' in reference to Kor. xl, 11: '*Thou hast caused us to die twice.*'

8. 'Thy foes,' etc., i.e. they will beguile thee with a form resembling mine at the moment when I manifest my essence to thee, i.e. thy desire to obtain possession of my essence will deceive thee and make thee imagine that the form in which I appear to thee is I myself.

9. 'I am in a guarded demesne,' etc., as it is said of the Prophet: '*for He causes a guard (of angels) to go before and behind him*' (Kor. lxxii, 27), that he might be in no doubt concerning his inspiration. This is the meaning of my verse, 'At night the angels descended upon my heart and circled it like the sphere that circles the pole-star.'

10. 'This poem of mine is without rhyme,' i.e. it has no recurring rhyme-letter (روىّ), which in a rhymed poem would invariably precede the ها.

'I intend by it only Her' (or, as the author expresses it, 'only the letter *há*'), i.e. 'I have no connexion except with Her, since my connexion with the phenomenal world is entirely for Her sake, in so far as She reveals Herself there.'

XLIII

1. Let me never forget my abode at Wána and my saying to camel-riders as they departed and arrived,
2. 'Stay beside us a while that we may be comforted thereby, for I swear by those whom I love that I am consoled (by thinking of you).'
3. If they set out they will journey with the most auspicious omen, and if they halt they will alight at the most bountiful halting-place.
4. 'Twas in the glen of the valley of Qanát I met them, and my last sight of them was between an-Naqá and al-Mushalshal.
5. They watch every place where the camels find pasturage, but they pay no heed to the heart of a lover led astray.
6. O camel-driver, have pity on a youth whom you see breaking colocynth when he bids farewell,
7. Laying his palms crosswise on his bosom to still a heart that throbbed at the noise of the (moving) howdah.
8. They say, 'Patience!' but grief is not patient. What can I do, since patience is far from me?
9. Even if I had patience and were ruled by it, my soul would not be patient. How, therefore, when I have it not?

Commentary

1. 'Wána,' i.e. the station of confession and shortcoming and failure to pay due reverence to the majesty of the Divine presence.

'Camel-riders,' i.e. the saints and favourites of God (الابرار والمقرّبين).

5. 'Every place where the camels find pasturage,' i.e. the objects to which our aspirations tend.

6. 'O camel-driver': he addresses the Divine voice which calls the aspirations towards it.

'Breaking colocynth,' i.e. having his face distorted with anguish (for when colocynth is broken its pungent smell causes the eyes to water). Imru'u'l-Qays says (cf. Ahlwardt, *The Dîwâns*, 204, No. 26):

كأنّى غداةَ البَيْنِ يَوْمَ تحمّلوا * لدى سَمُرات الحَيّ ناقِفُ حَنْظَلِ

XLIV

1. The full moon appeared in the night of hair, and the black narcissus bedewed the rose.
2. A tender girl is she: the fair women were confounded by her, and her radiance outshone the moon.
3. If she enters into the mind, that imagination wounds her: how, then, can she be perceived by the eye?
4. She is a phantom of delight that melts away when we think of her: she is too subtle for the range of vision.
5. Description sought to explain her, but she was transcendent, and description became dumb.
6. Whenever it tries to qualify her, it always retires baffled.
7. If one who seeks her will give rest to his beasts, others will not give rest to the beast of reflection.
8. She is a joy that transports from the rank of humanity every one who burns with love of her,
9. From jealousy that her clear essence should be mingled with the filth which is in the tanks.
10. She excels the sun in splendour: her form is not to be compared with any.
11. The heaven of light is under the sole of her foot: her diadem is beyond the spheres.

Commentary

1. 'The full moon,' etc., i.e. the Divine manifestation appeared in the unseen world of mysterious knowledge.

'And the black narcissus,' etc., i.e. the weeping eye bedewed the red cheeks. He means to say that the centre of Essential manifestation replenished the Divine names.

2. 'The fair women,' i.e. the attendant Names.

7. 'One who seeks her,' i.e. the gnostic who is aware that he cannot reach her.

'His beasts,' i.e. his aspirations.

'Others,' i.e. men of understanding who assert that God is known by logical demonstration.

8. 'Transports from the rank of humanity,' i.e. to the next world, in which the disembodied spirits assume different forms (مقام التحوّل فى الصور).

9. 'The filth which is in the tanks,' i.e. the impurity and darkness of nature in the corporeal world.

11. Cf. Kor. xx, 4, and the Tradition that God, before He created the Throne, was in a dense cloud, and neither above it nor beneath it was any air.

XLV

1. The loved ones of my heart—where are they? Say, by God, where are they?
2. As thou sawest their apparition, wilt thou show to me their reality?
3. How long, how long was I seeking them! and how often did I beg to be united with them,
4. Until I had no fear of being parted from them, and yet I feared to be amongst them.
5. Perchance my happy star will hinder their going afar from me,
6. That mine eye may be blest with them, and that I may not ask, 'Where are they?'

COMMENTARY

1. 'The loved ones,' i.e. the sublime spirits.

2. 'Their apparition,' i.e. their manifestation in the world of similitude.

4. 'I feared to be amongst them,' i.e. lest their radiance should consume me.

5. 'My happy star,' i.e. the Divine favour predestined to me.

XLVI

1. There is a war of love between the entrails and the large eyes, and because of that war the heart is in woe.
2. Dark-lipped and swart is she, her mouth honeyed: the

evidence of the bees is the white honey which they produce.

3. Full-ankled, a darkness o'er a moon; in her cheek a red blush; she is a bough growing on hills.
4. Beautiful, decked with ornaments; she is not wedded; she shows teeth like hailstones for lustre and coolness.
5. She keeps aloof in earnest, though she plays at loving in jest; and death lies between that earnest and jest.
6. Never did the night darken but there came, following it, the breath of dawn: 'tis known from of old.
7. And never do the East winds pass over meadows containing coy virgins with swelling breasts
8. But they bend the branches and whisper, as they blow, of the flowery scents which they carry.
9. I asked the East wind to give me news of them. The wind said, 'What need hast thou of the news?
10. I left the pilgrims in al-Abraqán and in Birk al-Ghimád and in Birk al-Ghamím near at hand;
11. They are not settled in any country.' I said to the wind, 'Where can they take refuge when the steeds of my desire are pursuing them?'
12. Far be the thought! They have no abode save my mind. Wherever I am, there is the full moon. Watch and see!
13. Is not my imagination her place of rising and my heart her place of setting? for the ill-luck of the *bán* and *gharab* trees hath ceased.
14. The raven does not croak in our encampments or make any rift in the harmony of our union.

Commentary

1. He says: 'There is a war of love between the world of intermixture and cohesion and the Divine Ideas, because this world desires and loves them inasmuch as its life is wholly derived from their beholding it. Nothing but this natural world hinders the hearts of gnostics from perceiving the Divine Ideas; accordingly the heart is in woe and distress because of the war that continually exists between them.'

2. 'Dark-lipped and swart is she': he refers to one of the Divine Ideas, whom he describes as having dark lips on account of the mysteries which she contains.

'The evidence of the bees': he mentions the bees because they have immediate experience of the inspiration which the hearts of gnostics desire.

3. 'Full-ankled,' i.e. mighty and terrible, with reference to يوم يكشف عن ساق (Kor. lxviii, 42) and to Kor. lxxv, 29.

'A darkness o'er a moon,' i.e. she is hidden save to the eye of contemplation.

'A bough growing on hills,' referring to the quality of self-subsistence (القيّومية) which is revealed in Divine manifestations.

4. 'Ornaments,' i.e. the Divine Names.

'Not wedded,' i.e. no human being has ever known her.

'Teeth like hailstones,' referring to the purity of her manifestation.

5. 'She keeps aloof in earnest,' i.e. she is really inaccessible.

'Death,' i.e. anguish for those who love her.

6. 'Never did the night darken,' etc., i.e. every esoteric mystery has its corresponding exoteric manifestation; God is both the Inward and the Outward.

7. 'The East winds,' i.e. the spiritual influences of Divine manifestation.

'Meadows,' i.e. hearts.

'Coy virgins,' etc., i.e. subtle forms of Divine wisdom and sensuous knowledge derived from the station of shame and beauty.

8. 'They bend the branches,' i.e. the Self-subsistent inclines towards those who subsist in phenomena.

11. 'No country in particular,' etc., i.e. they do not remain in any one state, referring to settlement in the station of change (التمكّن في مقام التلوين), which theosophists consider to be the most exalted of all the stations.

13. The *bán* tree suggests *bayn* (separation), and the *gharab* tree *ghurbat* (exile).

XLVII

1. O dove on the *bán* tree at Dhát al-Ghaḍá, I am oppressed by the burden thou hast laid upon me.
2. Who can support the anguish of love? Who can drain the bitter draught of destiny?
3. I say in my grief and burning passion, 'O would that he who caused my sickness had tended me when I am sick!'
4. He passed by the house-door mocking, hiding himself, veiling his head and turning away.
5. His veiling did me no hurt; I was only hurt by his having turned away from me.

Commentary

1. 'O dove,' i.e. the Absolute Wisdom.

'Dhát al-Ghaḍá,' referring to states of self-mortification.

'The burden': cf. Kor. xxxiii, 72.

4. 'He passed,' etc., referring to Divine thoughts which flash upon the mind and are gone in a moment.

5. i.e. I am necessarily veiled from God, but God's turning away from me is caused by some quality in me of which I am ignorant and which I cannot remove until God enables me to know what it is.

XLVIII

1. O camel-driver, turn aside at Sal' and halt by the *bán* tree of al-Mudarraj,
2. And call to them, imploring their pity and grace, 'O my princes, have ye any consolation?'
3. At Ráma, between an-Naqá and Ḥájir, is a girl enclosed in a howdah.
4. Oh, her beauty—the tender maid! Her fairness gives light like lamps to one travelling in the dark.
5. She is a pearl hidden in a shell of hair as black as jet,
6. A pearl for which reflection dives and remains unceasingly in the deeps of that ocean.
7. He who looks upon her deems her to be a gazelle of the

sand-hills because of her neck and the loveliness of her gestures.

8. 'Tis as though she were the morning sun in Aries, crossing the degrees of the zodiac at their farthest height.
9. If she lifts her veil or uncovers her face, she holds cheap the rays of the bright dawn.
10. I called to her, between the guarded pasture and Ráma, 'Who will help a man that alighted at Sal' in good hope?
11. Who will help a man lost in a desert, dismayed, confounded in his wits, miserable?
12. Who will help a man drowned in his tears, intoxicated by the wine of passion for those well-set teeth?
13. Who will help a man burned by his sighs, distraught by the beauty of those spacious eyebrows?'
14. The hands of Love have played at their will with his heart, and he commits no sin in that which he seeks.

Commentary

1. 'Halt by the *bán* tree of al-Mudarraj': he says, addressing the Divine messenger which calls the aspirations that seek to know and behold Him, 'Appear to me in the station of self-subsistence and lovingkindness gradually (على التدريج), not suddenly, lest I perish.'

2. 'And call to them,' i.e. to the Divine Names.

3. 'Ráma,' one of the stations of abstraction and isolation.

'Between an-Naqá and Ḥájir,' between the white hill and the most inaccessible veil, to which the hearts of mystics can never attain.

'A girl enclosed in a howdah,' i.e. the Essential Knowledge contained in the hearts of some gnostics.

4. 'To one travelling in the dark,' i.e. to those who ascend and journey in the night (like the Prophet).

6. God is beyond the reach of mental effort; He is revealed by Divine favour to a heart empty of all thoughts.

8. 'Crossing the degrees of the zodiac,' etc., in reference to the magnification and glory which the seer feels in himself as he continues to contemplate her.

10. 'Sal',' one of the stations of Divine sanctity.

12. 'In his tears,' i.e. in the knowledge that comes of contemplation.

'Wine,' i.e. every science that inspires joy and rapture in the human soul, e.g. the science of the Divine perfection.

'Those well-set teeth,' i.e. the grades of knowledge of God.

13. 'Those spacious eyebrows,' i.e. the station between the two Wazírs and Imáms. He alludes to the station of the Quṭb.

XLIX

1. Who will show me her of the dyed fingers? Who will show me her of the honeyed tongue?
2. She is one of the girls with swelling breasts who guard their honour, tender, virgin, and beautiful,
3. Full moons over branches: they fear no waning.
4. In a garden of my body's country is a dove perched on a *bán* bough,
5. Dying of desire, melting with passion, because that which befell me hath befallen her;
6. Mourning for a mate, blaming Time, who shot her unerringly, as he shot me.
7. Parted from a neighbour and far from a home! Alas, in my time of severance, for my time of union!
8. Who will bring me her who is pleased with my torment? I am helpless because of that with which she is pleased.

Commentary

1. 'Her of the dyed fingers': he means the phenomenal power (القدرة المحدثة) by which the Eternal power (القدرة القديمة) is hidden according to the doctrine of some scholastic theologians. He says, 'Who will impart to me the truth of this matter, so far as knowledge thereof is possible?' He wishes to know whether God manifests Himself therein (هل يصحّ فيها تجلٍّ) or not. The author denies such manifestation, but some mystics and the Mu'tazilites allow it, while the Ṣúfís among the Ash'arites leave the question undecided.

4. 'A dove,' etc., i.e. a spiritual Prophetic essence which appeared in the incommunicable self-subsistence. He refers to the belief of some Ṣúfís that Man cannot be invested with the Divine Self-subsistence (انّ القيّومية لا يتخلّق بها).

5. 'Dying of desire,' etc., with reference to Kor. iii, 29, '*Follow me, that God may love you,*' and Kor. v, 59, '*He loves them and they love Him.*'

6. 'A mate,' i.e. the Universal Form (الصورة الجامعة).

'Blaming Time,' because the forms belonging to the world of similitude are limited by Time in that world.

7. 'A neighbour,' i.e. a gnostic who became veiled from his Lord by his 'self' after having subsisted by his Lord and for the sake of his Lord.

'A home,' i.e. his natural constitution, whenever he returns to it.

L

1. Oh, the traitress! She has left bitten by her viper-like locks one who would fain approach her,
2. And she bends her soft eye and melts him and leaves him sick on his bed.
3. She shot the arrows of her glances from the bow of an eyebrow, and on whatever side I came I was killed.

Commentary

1. 'The traitress,' i.e. a deceitful Attribute, which caused one who sought her to become enamoured of the mysterious sciences derived from the Divine majesty and beauty.

2. 'His bed,' i.e. his body.

3. He describes the 'passing away' produced by contemplation of the Divine Ideas.

LI

1. At Dhát al-Aḍá and al-Ma'zimán and Báriq and Dhú Salam and al-Abraqán to the traveller by night
2. Appear flashes of swords from the lightnings of smiling mouths like musk-glands, the odour whereof none is permitted to smell.

3. If war is waged against them, they draw the swords of their glances; and if peace is made with them, they break the bonds of constraint.
4. They and we enjoyed two equal pleasures, for the Beloved has one kingdom and the lover another.

Commentary

1–2. He says, 'In the station of light and that of the soul's oppression between the two worlds and that of the manifestation of the Essence and that where the ascending spirits find peace (سلم) appears a terribly beguiling grace which is veiled by the favour of the Beloved.'

3. This verse refers to the Wrath and Mercy of God.

4. 'Equal,' because God created Man after His own image.

'For the Beloved,' etc., i.e. the lover and the Beloved exert a kind of mutual influence (تصرّف) upon one another.

LII

1. I am content with Raḍwá as a meadow and a lodging-place, for it has a pasture in which is cool water.
2. May be, those whom I love will hear of its fertility, so that they will take it as an abode and lodging-place.
3. For lo, my heart is attached to them and listens silently whenever the camel-driver urges them on with his chant.
4. And if they call to one another to set out and cross the desert, thou wilt hear its wailing behind their camels.
5. And if they make for az-Zawrá, it will be in front of them, and if they are bound for al-Jar'á, it will alight there.
6. No fortune is found except where they are and where they encamp, for the bird of Fortune has fledglings in their tribe.
7. Fear for myself and fear for her sake battled with each other, and neither gave way to its adversary.
8. When her splendours dazzle mine eyes, the sound of my sobbing deafens her ears.

COMMENTARY

1. 'Raḍwá,' with reference to the station of Divine satisfaction (مقام الرضا).

'A pasture,' i.e. spiritual nourishment.

2. 'Those whom I love,' i.e. gnostics like himself.

4. 'The desert,' i.e. the stations of abstraction (التجريد).

'Their camels,' i.e. the aspirations journeying away from the body.

5. 'Az-Zawrá,' i.e. the presence of the Quṭb.

'In front of them': he means that he anticipates them in his thoughts and wishes.

'Al-Jar'á,' i.e. a place where they suffer painful self-mortification.

6. The gnostic seeks only that which is akin to himself.

7. 'Fear for myself,' i.e. fear lest my eyes should be dazzled by the manifestation of my Beloved's glory.

'Fear for her sake,' i.e. fear lest her ears should be deafened by the noise of my sobbing.

LIII

1. Whenever we meet to take farewell thou wouldst deem us, as we clasp and embrace, to be a doubled letter.
2. Although our bodies are dual, the eye sees only a single one.
3. This is because of my leanness and his light, and were it not for my moaning, I should have been invisible to the eye.

COMMENTARY

1–2. The doubled letter is two letters, one of which is concealed in the other. The soul, bidding farewell to the body, says, 'We are in this case, for though we are really two, we appear to be one.' The soul loves the body because all her knowledge of God is gained through her imprisonment in the body and through her making use of it in order to serve God. The author also refers to the verse, 'I am he whom I love and he whom I love is I.'

The mention of 'farewell' indicates a distinction between the qualities which properly belong to the lover and those which properly belong to the Beloved.

3. 'My leanness,' i.e. I am of the spiritual world.

'And his light,' i.e. on account of the intensity of his light his eye cannot perceive either his own radiance or my subtlety.

'And were it not,' etc.: so Mutanabbí says, 'Were it not that I speak to thee, thou wouldst not see me.'

LIV

1. They said, 'The suns are in the heavenly sphere.' Where should the sun dwell but in heaven?
2. When a throne is set up, there must be a king to sit erect upon it.
3. When the heart is purged of its ignorance, then must the angel descend.
4. He made Himself master of me and I of Him, and each of us hath possessed the other.
5. My being His property is evident, and my possessing Him is (proved by) His saying, 'Come hither.'
6. O camel-driver, let us turn aside and do not lead the travellers past Dár al-Falak.
7. A house on a river-bank near al-Musanná caused thee to fall sick and did not make thee forget thy sickness.
8. Would that the lord of desire had laid on thee (O my censor!) my pain and the burden of love that was laid on me!
9. For neither Zarúd nor Ḥájir nor Salam is an abode that emaciated thee.
10. From the burning grief of the journey (towards Him) thou wert seeking the rain-clouds of union, but they did not o'ershadow thee.
11. The glory of His sovereignty abased thee, and would that as He abased thee so He had shown fondness towards thee!
12. And oh, would that, since in His pride He refused to show

Himself fond, oh, would that He had emboldened thee to show fondness towards Him!

Commentary

1. 'The suns are in the heavenly sphere,' i.e. the Divine radiance is in the heart.

2. Cf. Kor. xv, 29, and xx, 4.

3. 'The angel,' i.e. the most sublime spiritual essences.

4. 'He made Himself master of me,' inasmuch as I am limited by Him.

'And I of Him,' inasmuch as the Divine Names are manifested only in contingent being.

5. 'Come hither' (Kor. xii, 23), i.e. in order that the Names may be manifested, which is impossible unless I receive them.

6–7. 'Dár al-Falak,' a convent for pious women at Baghdád on the bank of the Tigris near al-Musanná, which is the residence of the Imám—on whom be peace! The author refers to the heart, because it is the Temple of Divine manifestation.

'Al-Musanná,' the station of the Quṭb, since it was the Caliph's palace.

'To fall sick,' i.e. to fall in love.

'And did not make thee forget thy sickness,' i.e. gave thee no relief.

9. He says that the passion of his soul was not kindled by anything contingent or finite.

11. He says: 'Although thou hadst knowledge of God, that knowledge did not humble thee so much as thou wert humbled by the glory of His manifestation, i.e. thy abasement was due to His glory, not to Himself; hence thy knowledge of Him was imperfect.'

LV

1. I am absent, and desire makes my soul die; and I meet him and am not cured, so 'tis desire whether I am absent or present.

2. And meeting with him creates in me what I never

imagined; and the remedy is a second disease of passion,

3. Because I behold a form whose beauty, as often as we meet, grows in splendour and majesty.
4. Hence there is no escape from a passion that increases in correspondence with every increase in his loveliness according to a predestined scale.

Commentary

1–4. He is continually tormented, for in the anguish of absence he hopes to be cured by meeting his Beloved, but the meeting only adds to his pain, because he is always moving from a lower state to a higher, and the latter inevitably produces in him a more intense passion than the former did.

LVI

1. (My goal is) the corniced palace of Baghdád, not the corniced palace of Sindád,[1]
2. The city set like a crown above the gardens, as though she were a bride who has been unveiled in the most fragrant chamber.
3. The wind plays with the branches and they are bent, and 'tis as though the twain had plighted troth with one another.
4. Meseems, Tigris is the string of pearls on her neck, and her spouse is our lord, the Imám who guides aright,
5. He who gives victory and is made victorious, the best of Caliphs, who in war does not mount on horseback.
6. God bless him! as long as a ringdove perched on a swaying bough shall moan for him,
7. And likewise as long as the lightnings shall flash of

[1] The second hemistich of this verse is borrowed from the verses of al-Aswad b. Ya'fur (*Mufaḍḍaliyyát*, ed. by Thorbecke, p. 52, 8–9; Bakrí, ed. by Wüstenfeld, 105):

ما ذا اؤمّل بعد آل محرّقٍ * تركوا منازلهم وبعد ايادِ
اهل الخورنق والسدير وبارقٍ * والقصرِ ذى الشرفات من سندادِ

Sindád was a palace of Ḥíra.

smiling mouths, for joy of which morning-showers flowed from mine eyes,

8. The mouths of virgins like the sun when the mists have withdrawn and when it shines forth clearly with most luminous radiance.

COMMENTARY

1. 'The corniced palace of Baghdád,' i.e. the presence of the Quṭb.

'The corniced palace of Sindád,' i.e. the kingdom of this world.

3. 'The wind plays with the branches,' i.e. the aspirations attach themselves to the Divine Self-subsistence, which inclines towards them.

4. 'Tigris,' i.e. the station of life.

'The Imám,' i.e. the Quṭb.

5. 'Who in war,' etc., i.e. he has quitted the body and taken his stand on the spiritual essence by which he is related to God.

6. 'A ringdove,' etc., i.e. the soul confined in the body.

7. 'As long as the lightnings,' etc., referring to the glories of Divine contemplation.

LVII

1. O breeze of the wind, bear to the gazelles of Najd this message: 'I am faithful to the covenant which ye know.'
2. And say to the young girl of the tribe, 'Our trysting-place is at the guarded pasture beside the hills of Najd on the Sabbath morn,
3. On the red hill towards the cairns and on the right hand of the rivulets and the solitary landmark.'
4. And if her words be true and she feel the same tormenting desire for me as I feel
5. For her, then we shall meet covertly in the heat of noon at her tent with the most inviolable troth,
6. And she and I will communicate what we suffer of love and sore tribulation and grievous pain.

7. Is this a vague dream or glad tidings revealed in sleep or the speech of an hour in whose speech was my happy fortune?
8. Perchance he who brought the objects of desire (into my heart) will bring them face to face with me, and their gardens will bestow on me the gathered roses.

Commentary

1. 'O breeze of the wind,' i.e. the subtle spiritual sense which gnostics use as a medium of communication.

'The gazelles of Najd,' i.e. the exalted spirits.

2. 'The young girl of the tribe,' i.e. the spirit especially akin to himself.

3. 'The red hill,' i.e. the station of beauty, since red is the fairest of all the colours.

'The solitary landmark,' i.e. the Divine singleness (الفردانية), which is inferior to oneness (الاحدية).

5. 'In the heat of noon,' i.e. in the station of equilibrium (الاستواء).

7. 'Is this a vague dream?' (cf. Kor. xii, 44), i.e. this union is impossible, for my spirit cannot escape from the corporeal world.

LVIII

1. Oh, is there any way to the damsels bright and fair? And is there anyone who will show me their traces?
2. And can I halt at night beside the tents of the curving sand? And can I rest at noon in the shade of the *arák* trees?
3. The tongue of inward feeling spoke, informing me that she says, 'Wish for that which is attainable.'
4. My love for thee is whole, O thou end of my hopes, and because of that love my heart is sick.
5. Thou art exalted, a full moon rising over the heart, a moon that never sets after it hath risen.
6. May I be thy ransom, O thou who art glorious in beauty and pride! for thou hast no equal amongst the fair.
7. Thy gardens are wet with dew and thy roses are blooming,

and thy beauty is passionately loved: it is welcome to all.

8. Thy flowers are smiling and thy boughs are fresh: wherever they bend, the winds bend towards them.

9. Thy grace is tempting and thy look piercing: armed with it the knight, affliction, rushes upon me.

COMMENTARY

1. 'The damsels bright and fair,' i.e. the knowledge derived from the manifestations of His Beautiful Name.

2. 'The tents of the curving sand,' i.e. the stations of Divine favour.

'The shade of the *arák* trees,' i.e. contemplation of the pure and holy Presence.

3. This station is gained only by striving and sincere application, not by wishing. 'Travel that thou mayst attain' (أسْلُكْ تَصِلْ).

5. 'A moon that never sets,' etc.: he points out that God never manifests Himself to anything and then becomes veiled from it afterwards.

7. 'Thy gardens are wet with dew,' i.e. all Thy creatures are replenished by the Divine qualities which are revealed to them.

'Thy roses are blooming,' in reference to a particular manifestation which destroys every blameworthy quality.

'It is welcome,' i.e. it is loved for its essence (محبوب لذاته).

8. 'Thy flowers,' etc., i.e. Thy knowledge is welcome to the heart.

'Thy boughs,' i.e. the spiritual influences which convey Thy knowledge (حاملاتها منك).

LIX

1. Ṭayba hath a gazelle from whose witching eye (glances like) the edge of a keen blade are drawn,

2. And at 'Arafát I perceived what she desired and I was not patient,

3. And on the night of Jam' we had union with her, such as is mentioned in the proverb.

4. The girl's oath is false: do not confide in that which betrays.
5. The wish I gained at Miná, would that it might continue to the last hour of my life!
6. In La'la' I was transported with love for her who displays to thee the splendour of the bright moon.
7. She shot Ráma and inclined to dalliance at aṣ-Ṣabá and removed the interdiction at al-Ḥájir.
8. And she watched a lightning-gleam over Báriq with a glance swifter than a thought that passes in the mind.
9. And the waters of al-Ghaḍá were diminished by a blazing fire which passion kindled within his ribs.
10. And she appeared at the *bán* tree of an-Naqá and chose (for her adornment) the choicest of its superb hidden pearls.
11. And at Dhát al-Aḍá she turned backward in dread of the lurking lion.
12. At Dhú Salam she surrendered my life-blood to her murderous languishing glance.
13. She stood on guard at the guarded pasture and bent at the sand-bend, swayed by her all-cancelling decisive resolution.
14. And at 'Álij she managed her affair (in such a way) that she might escape from the claw of the bird.
15. Her Khawarnaq rends the sky and towers beyond the vision of the observer.

Commentary

1. 'Ṭayba (Medina) hath a gazelle,' referring to a Muḥammadan degree (مرتبة محمّدية), i.e. a spiritual presence belonging to the station of Muḥammad.

3. 'On the night of Jam'': he says, 'we abode in the station of proximity (القربة) and He concentrated me upon myself' (جمعنى علىّ).

'In the proverb,' namely, 'He did not salute until he bade farewell' (ما سلّم حتى ودّع), i.e. they parted as soon as they met.

4. He says, 'Put no trust in an Attribute that is not self-subsistent and depends on One who may not always accomplish its desires.'

7. 'She shot Ráma,' i.e. she shot that which she was seeking (رمت ما كانت ترومه), because she regarded the thing as being the opposite of what it was and of what she believed it to be.

'And inclined to dalliance at aṣ-Ṣabá,' i.e. she desired to manifest herself.

8. 'A lightning-gleam,' i.e. a *locus* of manifestation for the Essence.

10. 'And chose,' etc., i.e. she revealed herself in the most lovely shape.

11. 'Dhát al-Aḍá,' i.e. the place of illumination.

'She turned backward,' etc., i.e. she returned to her natural world for fear that that fierce light should consume her.

12. Gnostics are annihilated by their vision of the Truth, but this does not happen to the vulgar, because they lack knowledge of themselves.

13. 'The guarded pasture,' i.e. the station of Divine glory.

'Bent,' i.e. inclined with Divine mercy. This refers to her investing herself with Divine qualities (التخلّق).

14. 'That she might escape,' etc., i.e. she was unwilling to receive from the spirits, for she wished to receive only from God, by intuitive feeling (ذوقًا), not by cognition (علمًا). God sometimes bestows His gifts by the mediation of the exalted spirits, and sometimes immediately.

15. 'Her Khawarnaq,' i.e. the seat of her kingdom.

LX

1. Approach the dwelling of dear ones who have taken covenants — may clouds of incessant rain pour upon it! —
2. And breathe the scent of the wind over against their land, in desire that the (sweet) airs may tell thee where they are.

3. I know that they encamped at the *bán* tree of Iḍam, where the *'arár* plants grow and the *shíḥ* and the *katam.*

COMMENTARY

1. Dear ones,' i.e. the exalted spirits.

Covenants,' i.e. the Divine covenants taken from the spirits of the prophets.

Clouds of incessant rain,' i.e. knowledge descending upon them continuously.

2. And breathe,' etc., referring to the Tradition, 'I feel the breath of the Merciful from the quarter of Yemen.'

3. 'I know.' The author says that ظنّ is here used with the meaning of علم.

At the *bán* tree of Iḍam,' i.e. the station of Absolute purity at the end of the journey to God.

'The *'arár* plants,' etc., i.e. sweet spiritual influences proceeding from lovely spiritual beings.

LXI

1. O *bán* tree of the valley, on the bank of the river of Baghdád!
2. A mournful dove that cooed on a swaying bough filled me with grief for thee.
3. His plaintive song reminds me of the plaintive song of the lady of the chamber.
4. Whenever she tunes her triple chords, thou must forget the brother of al-Hádí.
5. And if she lavishes her melody, who is Anjasha the camel-driver?
6. I swear by Dhu 'l-Khaḍimát and then by Sindád
7. That I am passionately in love with Salmá who dwells at Ajyád.
8. No; I am mistaken: she dwells in the black clot of blood in the membrane of my liver.
9. Beauty is confounded by her, and odours of musk and saffron are scattered abroad.

Commentary

1. 'O *bán* tree,' etc., i.e. the tree of light in the station of the Quṭb.

2. 'A mournful dove,' i.e. an exalted spirit.

'On a swaying bough,' i.e. the human organism in the station of self-subsistence (النشأة الانسانية فى مقام القيّومية).

3. 'The lady of the chamber,' i.e. every reality that exercises dominion in its own world.

4. 'Her triple chords,' i.e. the body, with its three dimensions, viz. length, breadth, and depth. 'Triple chords' may also refer to the grades of the three Names, which are the abode of the two Imáms and the Quṭb.

'Al-Hádí,' the 'Abbásid Caliph. His brother was a fine musician.

5. 'Anjasha,' a camel-driver contemporary with the Prophet. He used to chant so sweetly that the camels died. (See Nawawí, ed. by Wüstenfeld, 164.)

7. 'Salmá' (a woman's name), i.e. a Solomonic station.

'Ajyád' (plural of جيد, neck), a place at Mecca. Here it refers to the throat through which the breath passes.

ERRATA

Page 76, line 6. *For* al-Naqá *read* an-Naqá.
p. 77, l. 2. ,, ,,
p. 89, l. 10. *For* al-Dharíḥ *read* adh-Dharíḥ.
p. 91, l. 23. For *hádí* read *ḥádí*.
p. 104, l. 18. *For* al-Naqá *read* an-Naqá.
p. 105, ll. 13, 21. ,, ,,
p. 110, l. 23. ,, ,,
p. 121, l. 11. *For* white clouds *read* rain-clouds

INDEX

I. PERSONS, PLACES, AND BOOKS

Names of persons and places are printed in Roman type, whether they occur in the translation or in that portion of the Arabic text which has not been translated. Titles of books are printed in italics.

II. SUBJECTS AND TECHNICAL TERMS